ENGLISH in Common 1B

Student Book/Workbook with ActiveBook

Jonathan Bygrave

Series Consultants
María Victoria Saumell and Sarah Louisa Birchley

ALWAYS LEARNING

PEARSON

English in Common 1B
Student Book/Workbook Split Edition

Pearson Education, 10 Bank Street, White Plains, NY 10606

Staff credits: The editorial, design, production, and manufacturing people who make up the *English in Common 1* team are Margaret Antonini, Allen Ascher, Rhea Banker, Eleanor Kirby Barnes, Mike Boyle, Tracey Cataldo, Aerin Csigay, Dave Dickey, Chris Edmonds, Mike Kemper, Loretta Steeves, Leigh Stolle, Katherine Sullivan, and Charlie Green.

This series is dedicated to Charlie Green. Without Charlie's knowledge of pedagogy, strong work ethic, sense of humor, patience, perseverance, and creativity, *English in Common* would never have existed.

Cover design: Tracey Cataldo
Cover photo: © qushe/shutterstock.com
Text design: Tracey Cataldo
Text composition: TSI Graphics
Text font: MetaPlus

ISBN 13: 978-0-13-262861-7
ISBN 10: 0-13-262861-9

Library of Congress Cataloging-in-Publication Data
Bygrave, Jonathan
English in common. Book 1 / Jonathan Bygrave.
p. cm.
ISBN 0-13-247003-9—ISBN 0-13-262725-6—
ISBN 0-13-262727-2—ISBN 0-13-262728-0—
ISBN 0-13-262729-9—ISBN 0-13-262731-0
1. English language—Textbooks for foreign speakers.
2. English language—Grammar.
3. English language—Spoken English.
PE1128.B865 2011
428.24--dc23

2011024736

Photo Credits–Student Book: All photos are used under license from Shutterstock.com except for the following: p. 62 (left) Pearson Education, (right) Pearson Education; p. 67 (1) iStockphoto.com; p. 69 (A) Todd Warnock/Corbis, (C) iStockphoto.com; p. 80 (bottom middle) iStockphoto.com, (middle right) Dreamstime.com, (bottom right) Dreamstime.com; p. 85 Blend Images/Getty Images; p. 89 (A) Al Bello/Getty Images, (B) Bettmann/Corbis, (C) ERMA/Retna Ltd., (D) AP Images/David Brauchli; p. 90 (A) AP Images/Doug Pizac, (B) AP Images/Mark Lennihan, (C) Michael Ochs Archives/Getty Images, (D) Ronald Grant Archive; p. 91 (left) Everett Collection Inc/Alamy, (right) Rex Features; p. 92 (middle) Dreamstime.com; p. 93 (right) Jeremy Sutton-Hibbert/Alamy; p. 105 (2) Ariel Skelley/Getty Images, (3) iStockphoto.com; p. 113 (1) iStockphoto.com.

Photo Credits–Workbook: p. 37 (left) Leland Bobbe/Corbis, (right) PunchStock, (middle) PunchStock, Shutterstock.com; p. 39 (left) PunchStock, (right) Shutterstock.com; p. 40 Jim Graigmyle/Corbis; p. 45 Shutterstock.com; p. 47 (A) Shutterstock.com, (B) Shutterstock.com, (C) PunchStock; p. 51 (top left) TIPS Images, (bottom left) Shutterstock.com, (right) SuperStock; p. 52 Work Book Stock/Getty Images; p. 53 Shutterstock.com; p. 54 (top) PunchStock, (bottom) Dominic Dibbs/Anthony Blake Photo Library; p. 55 Iconica/Getty Images; p. 56 (top right) Hulton Archive/Getty Images, (middle right) V&A Images; p. 57 Bettmann/Corbis; p. 58 Rex Features; p. 62 (1) Neil Guegan/Corbis, (2) Reuters, (3) DK Images, (4) Ian M. Butterfield/Alamy; p. 63 (left) The Bridgeman Art Library Ltd/Self Portrait, 1887 (oil on canvas), Gogh, Vincent van (1853–90)/Musée d'Orsay, Paris, France, (right) The Bridgeman Art Library Ltd/Breton Peasants, 1894 (oil on canvas), Gauguin, Paul (1848–1903)/Lauros/Giraudon, Musée d'Orsay, Paris, France; p. 64 Press Association Images; p. 65 (top) PunchStock; p. 67 iStockphoto.com.

Illustration Credits–Student Book: Pages 110, 112 90 Grados; p. 70 Beach; p. 87 Grupa Smacnego; pp. 61, 62, 72 Andy Hammond (illustration.webb); pp. 79, 80, 111 Tim Kahane; p. 64 Gary Kaye; pp. 69, 82, 94 Sylvie Pinsonneaux (Eye Candy Illustration Agency); pp. 75, 85 Alan Rowe; pp. 111, 118 Technical Art services; p. 95 Lucy Truman; p. 70 Mark Watkinson (illustration.webb).

Illustration Credits–Workbook: Beach; F&L Productions; Gary Kaye; Graham Kennedy; Joanne Kerr (New Division); Lucy Truman (New Division); Mark Duffin; Roger Penwill.

Printed in the United States of America
6 7 8 9 10—V082—16 15 14

Contents

English in Common is a six-level course that helps adult and young-adult English learners develop effective communication skills that correspond to the Common European Framework of Reference for Languages (CEFR). Every level of *English in Common* is correlated to a level of the CEFR, and each lesson is formulated around a specific CAN DO objective.

English in Common 1 has ten units. Each unit has ten pages.

There are three two-page lessons in each unit.

A two-page Unit Wrap Up and a Reference page end each unit.

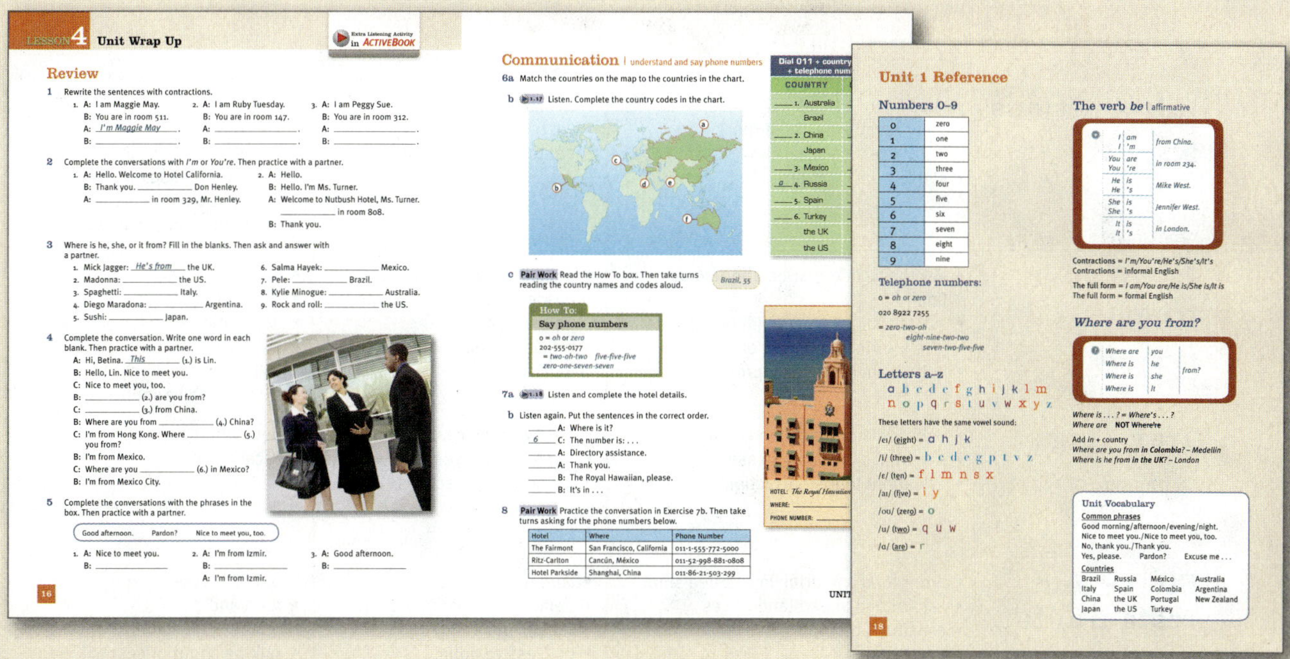

Back of Student Book

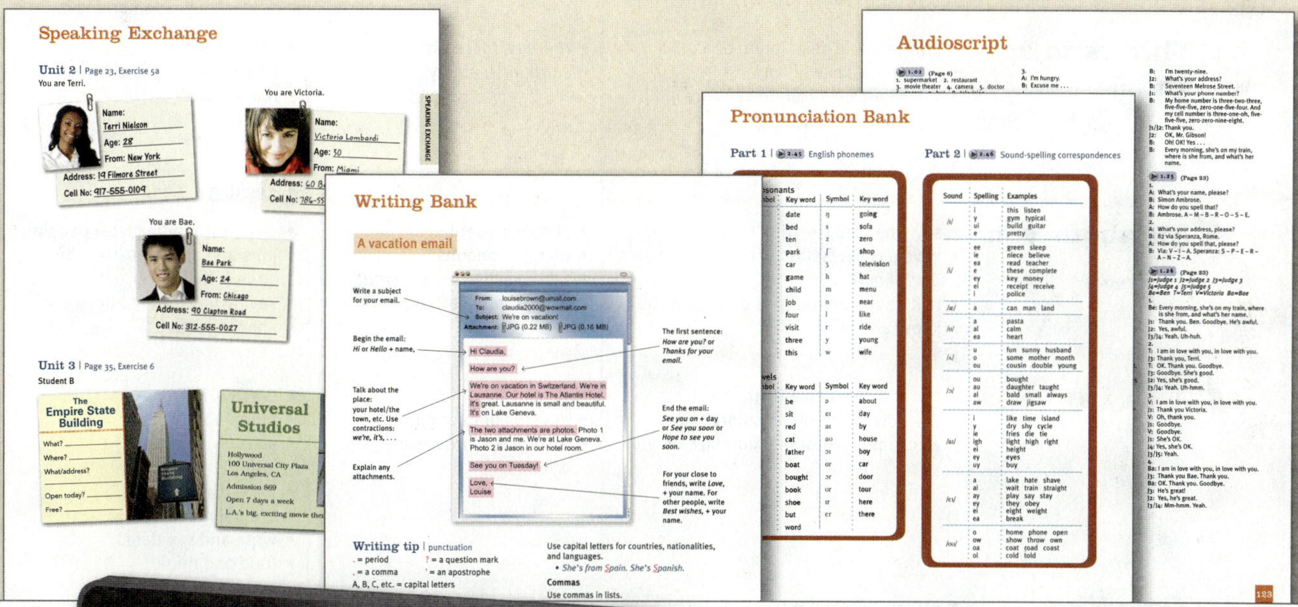

- Each Student Book contains an ***ActiveBook***, which provides the Student Book in digital format. *ActiveBook* also includes the complete Audio Program and Extra Listening activities.
- An optional **MyEnglishLab** provides students with the opportunity for extra practice anytime, anywhere.
- The Teacher's Resource Book contains teaching notes, photocopiable extension activities, and an ***ActiveTeach***, which provides a digital Student Book enhanced by interactive whiteboard software. *ActiveTeach* also includes the videos and video activities, as well as the complete Test Bank.

READING/WRITING	LISTENING	COMMUNICATION/ PRONUNCIATION
Reading texts: • an airport arrivals board • an ad for vacations • hotel contact information **Writing task:** conversation completion	**Listening tasks:** • identify situations • place in sequence • identify room numbers and phone numbers • determine nationalities	**Communication:** understand and say phone numbers **Pronunciation:** • alphabet • syllable recognition • sentence stress
Reading texts: • an efriends profile • a family tree **Writing task:** a brief personal profile	**Listening tasks:** • determine relationships • perceive personal details • correct addresses • identify occupations	**Communication:** talk about favorite people and things **Pronunciation:** word stress in numbers
Reading texts: • an email about a New York vacation • advertisements for tourist attractions **Writing task:** a simple vacation email	**Listening tasks:** • discern details • identify subject pronouns • recognize the main ideas	**Communication:** have an extended phone conversation **Pronunciation:** plural "s"
Reading texts: • menus • information about a shopping district • an email **Writing task:** a paragraph about a shopping area	**Listening tasks:** • recognize the main idea • identify details • determine prices • identify situations • detect specific words	**Communication:** ask for and give locations **Pronunciation:** linking
Reading texts: • a short article about Washington D.C. • a map • a class schedule • job ads **Writing task:** a paragraph about a favorite place to visit	**Listening tasks:** • understand directions • identify the gist • distinguish abilities • recognize key information	**Communication:** check in to a bed and breakfast **Pronunciation:** vowel clarity in *can* and *can't*
Reading texts: • personal profiles • brief essays about friends and family • an email • a web questionnaire and key **Writing task:** a paragraph about a friend/family member	**Listening tasks:** • understand the gist • identify likes and dislikes • identify people • distinguish between true and false information	**Communication:** ask and answer questions about a friend **Pronunciation:** *yes/no* questions: intonation
Reading texts: • an article about a teacher's typical day • a questionnaire • a short handwritten note • a calendar **Writing task:** a note making a request	**Listening tasks:** • identify situations • recognize key phrases • recognize key information • understand location	**Communication:** get and give directions in a building **Pronunciation:** word stress
Reading texts: • a technology quiz • a scoring key • a restaurant menu **Writing task:** an email to a hotel	**Listening tasks:** • understand the gist • identify places • recognize key words	**Communication:** ask for and give information about people **Pronunciation:** reduction of sounds: *want to*
Reading texts: • biographies of famous people • an article about househusbands **Writing task:** a paragraph about your first teacher	**Listening tasks:** • understand the gist • identify key words • recognize situations	**Communication:** talk about school days **Pronunciation:** sentence stress
Reading texts: • a three-part article about a famous painting • short articles about good and bad news • a list of sales prices **Writing task:** a journal entry about a good/bad week	**Listening tasks:** • distinguish between true and false information • determine prices • understand main ideas	**Communication:** talk about past and future vacations **Pronunciation:** simple past *-ed* endings

UNIT 6
All about you

A

B

C

D

Warm Up

1a ▶ 2.02 Listen to the adjectives in the box and repeat. Then check the meanings in a dictionary.

sad	thin	tall	short	heavy	good-looking	young
old	rich	ugly	poor	happy	intelligent	

b **Pair Work** Say a word. Your partner says the opposite. *Short.* *Tall.*

2a Write the sentences in the box on the correct line.

He's not very rich.	He's rich.	He's very rich.	~~He's pretty rich.~~

+++ ________ ++ ________ + *He's pretty rich.* − ________

b **Pair Work** Talk about the photos. Use the adjectives with *very, pretty,* or *not very.*

LESSON 1

Say what you like/don't like

GRAMMAR simple present: *I/you;* object pronouns

Listening

1a 2.03 Listen. What's João's favorite kind of music?

American English	British English
soccer	*football*

b Listen again. What does João like? Write ✓ or ✗ next to each word or phrase.

____ 1. Chicago ____ 3. Brazilian music ____ 5. Indian food ____ 7. German cars
____ 2. soccer ____ 4. hip hop music ____ 6. French food ____ 8. Italian fashion

Grammar | simple present: *I like*

2a Complete the Active Grammar box with *do* or *don't*.

b Complete the sentences with *like* or *don't like*.

1. ☹ I *don't like* chicken.
2. ☺ I ____________ Los Angeles.
3. ☹ I ____________ Mondays.
4. ☺ I ____________ vacations.

Active Grammar

+	I	like	German cars.
–	I	don't like	hip hop music.
?	_____ you	like	soccer?
	Yes, I _____.		No, I _____.

See Reference page 68

c Write questions for each of the sentences above.

1. *Do you like chicken?*
2. ____________________
3. ____________________
4. ____________________

Pronunciation | *yes/no* questions: intonation

3a 2.04 Listen. Does the intonation go up (↗) or down (↘) at the end?

b Listen again. Repeat.

Speaking

4 **Pair Work** Think of one thing or person you like and one thing or person you don't like for each category. Tell your partner and ask if he or she likes it.

- food
- famous people
- sports teams
- cars
- music
- time of day
- colors
- places

I like Italian food. Do you like Italian food?

Yes, I do. I don't like salad. Do you like salad?

Grammar | object pronouns: *me/you/him/her/it/us/them*

5a 2.05 Match a sentence to a picture. Then listen and check your answers.

a. I don't like her.
b. ~~Do you like me?~~
c. I like them.
d. I don't like him.
e. I like you.
f. I like it.

1. *b*

2. ____

3. ____

4. ____

5. ____

6. ____

b Complete the chart with the underlined words in Exercise 5a.

Subject pronoun	Object pronoun	Subject pronoun	Object pronoun
I		*we*	*us*
you			
he/she/it		*they*	

Speaking

6a Read the How To box.

b Work in pairs.

Student A: Look at the list below.

Student B: Look at the list on page 111 in the Speaking Exchange.

1. Tom Cruise
2. Salma Hayek
3. beautiful beaches
4. department stores
5. instant coffee
6. Brad Pitt and Angelina Jolie
7. golf
8. baseball

How To:

Say when you don't understand

A: *Do you like Salma Hayek?*
B: *Sorry?/Pardon?/Who's Salma Hayek?*
A: *She's an actress.*
B: *Oh, yes. I like her.*

c Read your list to your partner. Your partner says *I like/don't like* + object pronoun.

Tom Cruise.

I don't like him.

7 **Pair Work** Do a 60-second interview with your partner. Use your questions from Exercise 4. Think of eight new questions. Use:

Do you like . . . ?

Who's/What's your favorite . . . ?

Have a conversation with someone you don't know

CAN DO

GRAMMAR simple present: *we/they; wh-* questions: *who/what/where*

Vocabulary | jobs and activities

1a Match the jobs in the box to the pictures.

____ architect	____ fashion designer	____ reporter
____ sales rep	____ construction worker	____ chef

a. 
b. 
c. 
d. 
e. 
f. 

b 2.06 Write a verb from the box below in each blank. Then listen and check your answers.

sell   write   build   cook   design (x2)

1. Architects *design* buildings.
2. Sales reps __________ things.
3. Fashion designers __________ clothes.
4. Reporters __________ articles.
5. Chefs __________ food.
6. Construction workers __________ buildings.

Listening

2a 2.07 Listen to four people at a hotel in China. Match the jobs from Exercise 1a to the people in the photo.

b Listen again. Mark the sentences true (*T*) or false (*F*).

Sharon and Pat

____ 1. They live in the US.
____ 2. They are there on business.
____ 3. They design houses and office buildings.

Catherine and Anthony

____ 4. They are there on vacation.
____ 5. They live in Canada.
____ 6. PDS Fashions is a small company.

Grammar 1 | simple present: *we/they*

3a Complete the Active Grammar box with *do* or *don't*.

b Are the sentences below true for you? Write *Yes* or *No* next to them.

____ 1. I like American movies.
____ 2. I like Italian food.
____ 3. I like British music.
____ 4. I live near this school.
____ 5. I like soccer.
____ 6. I like sushi.

Active Grammar

+	*We/They*		*design*	*houses.*
−	*We/They*		*____ live*	*in Canada.*
?	*Do*	*we/they*	*sell*	*computers?*
	Yes, we/they ____. No, we/they ____.			

See Reference page 68

c **Pair Work** Make sentences about things that are true for both you and your partner.

We both don't like American movies.

Grammar 2 | *wh-* questions: *who/what/where*

4 Complete the Active Grammar box with *Who, What,* or *Where.*

5 Write questions from the Active Grammar box for each answer below.

1. A: *What do you do*____?
   B: I'm a designer.
2. A: ____________?
   B: I work in Paris.
3. A: ____________?
   B: I work for GT Designs.
4. A: ____________?
   B: I design cars.

Active Grammar

What	*do*	*you*	*do?*
____	*do*	*you*	*work/live?*
____	*do*	*you*	*sell/design/write?*
____	*do*	*you*	*work for?*

See Reference page 68

6 **Pair Work** Read the How To box. Stand and ask other students questions from the Active Grammar box.

How To:

Show interest

A: *I'm a fashion designer/sales rep, etc.*
B: *Oh really?/Great!/Interesting. What do you build/design/sell, etc.?*

Speaking

7 **SPEAKING EXCHANGE** Work in groups of four as two pairs.

Students A and B: Read your details on page 109.

Students C and D: Read your details on page 111.

You are at a club in San Francisco. Have a conversation with the other pair. Use the questions from the Active Grammar box.

Talk about the routines of people you know

CAN DO

GRAMMAR simple present: *he/she/it*; short answers

Vocabulary | daily activities

1a Read the sentences. Write the correct underlined verb phrase under each picture.

1. I get up at 11 o'clock.
2. I take a shower every day.
3. I eat hamburgers for dinner.
4. I start work at nine.
5. I finish work at nine o'clock.
6. I eat a salad for breakfast.
7. I watch TV at night.
8. I don't go to bed early.

a. 

1. get up ________

b. 

____

c. 

____

d. 

____

e. 

____

f. 

____

g. 

____

h. 

____

b **Pair Work** Change the sentences in Exercise 1a to make them true for you. Tell your partner.

I get up at seven.

Reading

2a Read Emma's essay. Complete the sentences.

1. Mei is Emma's ________.
2. Frank is Emma's ________.
3. Roberta is Emma's ________.
4. Adam is Emma's ________.

b **Pair Work** Ask and answer questions with *Yes, he/she does*, or *No, he/she doesn't*.

1. Does Frank take a shower every day?
2. Does Adam get up at eight o'clock?
3. Does Mei eat fast food?
4. Does Roberta start work at eight thirty?
5. Does Frank eat fast food for breakfast?
6. Does Mei watch TV?

Emma

Mei is my best friend. She's a yoga teacher. She's not rich, but she's happy. She eats salad every day. She doesn't eat fast food, and she doesn't watch TV.

Frank is my brother and he's a biker. He's pretty tall and very intelligent. He eats fast food for breakfast every day. He doesn't take a shower every day.

Roberta is my aunt. She's a sales rep. She starts work at eight thirty in the morning, and she finishes work at nine o'clock at night. She's not a happy person.

Adam is a musician. He gets up at 11 o'clock in the morning, and he goes to bed at 2 o'clock in the morning. He's not very intelligent — but it's OK — he's good-looking and he's my husband. I love him!

Grammar | simple present: *he/she/it*

3 Look at Emma's essay in Exercise 2a on page 64 again. Complete the Active Grammar box.

Active Grammar

+	*He/She/It*		*start__*	*work at eight thirty.*
			finish__	*work at nine o'clock.*
–	*He/She/It*		*______ eat*	*fast food.*
			______ like	*salad.*
?	*Does*	*he*	*get up*	*at nine?*
		she	*eat*	*breakfast early?*
	Yes, he/she/it does. No, he/she/it doesn't.			

See Reference page 68

4a Complete the paragraph with the correct form of the words in the box.

start   get   like   ~~work~~   finish   watch   eat (x2)

My best friend is Koji. He's a chef in a French restaurant. He *works* (1.) in the evening, so he __________ (2.) up around ten or eleven o'clock in the morning. He __________ (3.) breakfast and lunch together – it's called "brunch". He __________ (4.) TV in the afternoon, and he __________ (5.) work around four o'clock. He __________ (6.) dinner at work. He __________ (7.) work around midnight. He __________ (8.) his job.

Koji

b Fill in the blanks with the correct form of the words in parentheses.

1. He *doesn't* *like* this music. (not like)
2. __________ they __________ here? (work)
3. What __________ he __________? (do)
4. Sarah __________ __________ a lot of emails. (not write)

Writing

5a Complete each sentence below with the name of a friend or family member.

1. ______________ is my best friend.
2. ______________ is my favorite family member.

b Make notes about each person.

- What does he or she do? (**Ex:** He's a teacher.)
- What adjectives describe him or her? (**Ex:** She's young, happy.)
- What are his or her routines? (**Ex:** He gets up at eight o'clock.)

c Look at the Writing Bank on page 116. Write a paragraph about each person above.

Extra Listening Activity in ACTIVEBOOK

Review

1 Complete each sentence or question with *me, you, him, her, it, us,* or *them.*

1. She's really nice. Do you like *her*?
2. I don't like this show. Do you like ___________?
3. Bill and Jenny aren't my friends. I don't like ___________.
4. I really like him, but I don't think he likes ___________.
5. You are great! I think he likes ___________.
6. He's my friend. I like ___________.
7. We like them, but do they like ___________?

2 Complete the questions with *What, Where,* or *Who.* Then work with a partner and ask and answer the questions with true information.

1. A: *Where* do you live?
   B: In San Francisco.
2. A: ___________ do you work for?
   B: A small software company.
3. A: ___________ do you do?
   B: I'm a sales rep.
4. A: ___________ do you sell?
   B: I sell computer software.
5. A: ___________ do you work?
   B: In Silicon Valley.

3 Fill in the blanks with the correct form of the verb in parentheses.

Hi Victor,

How are you? I'm fine, but my new roommate is a problem. His name is Oscar. He's a designer. He *designs* (1. design/✓) shoes. He *doesn't get up* (2. get up/✗) until 11 o'clock every day. He ___________ (3. take a shower/✗). He ___________ (4. eat/✗) breakfast, but he ___________ (5. watch/✓) TV for two or three hours. Then he ___________ (6. start/✓) work at about two o'clock in the afternoon. He ___________ (7. work/✗) in an office— he ___________ (8. work/✓) at home. He ___________ (9. finish/✓) work at about six o'clock. That's just four hours! He ___________ (10. go/✓) to bed at three o'clock in the morning.

What can I do?

Love, Julia

4 Use the words to write complete sentences.

1. I/not like/French food
   I don't like French food.
2. She/get up/at 8 o'clock
   ___________.
3. they/start work/early
   ___________?
4. Thomas/not eat/salad
   ___________.
5. Kim/watch TV/every day
   ___________?
6. Paul and I/write/articles for *Newsmag*
   ___________.
7. Where/Carlos/live
   ___________?
8. Jo and Alex/not go to bed/late
   ___________.

Communication | ask and answer questions about a friend

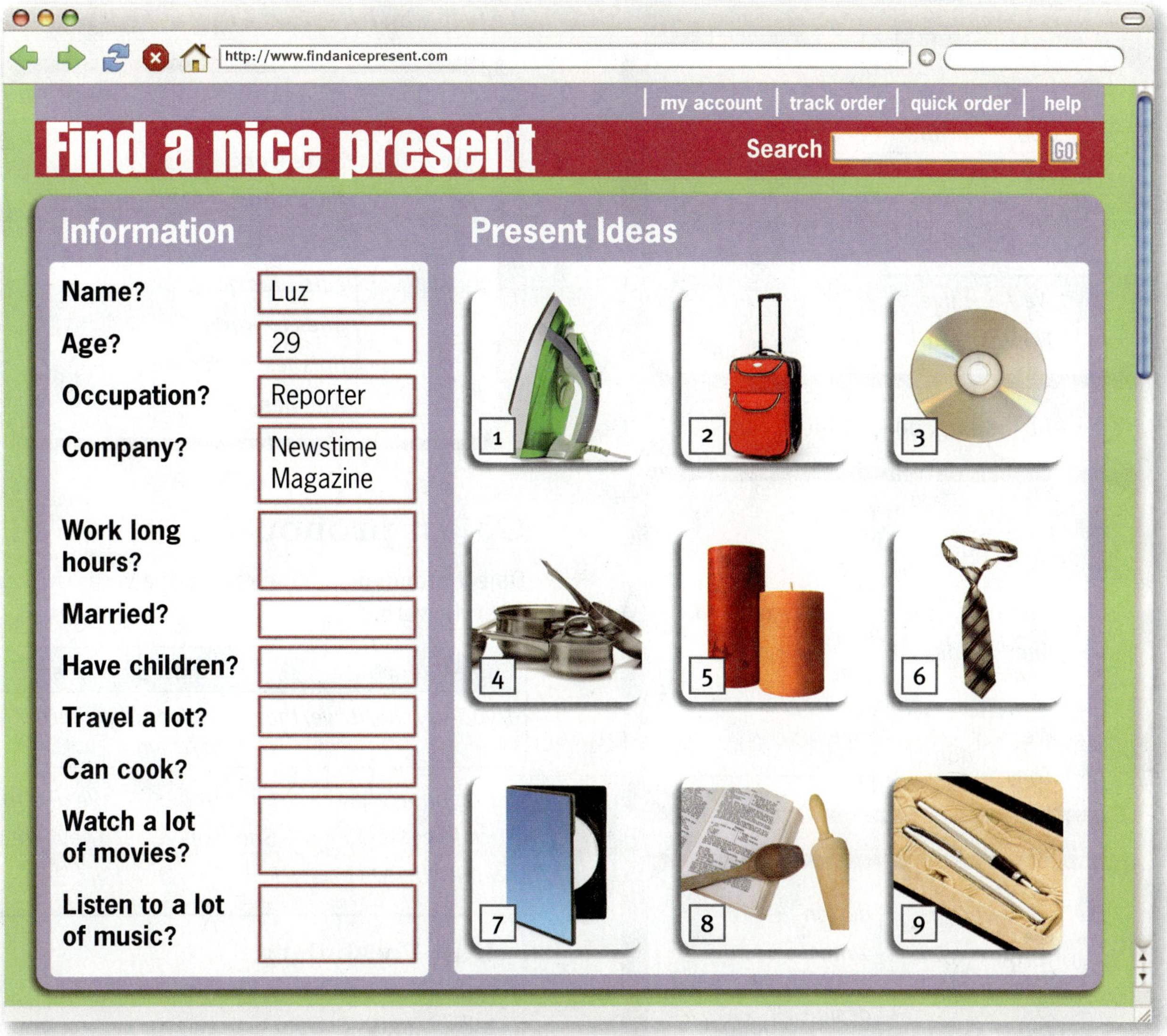

5 Match nine words in the box to the pictures on the website above.

___ tie	___ DVD	___ book	___ flowers	___ suitcase	___ MP3 player	___ cookbook
___ CD	___ bag	___ pens	___ wallet	___ candles	___ travel iron	___ saucepans

6 ▶2.08 Listen to Part 1 of the conversation. What is the problem?

7a ▶2.09 Listen to Part 2 of the conversation. Answer the questions on the website for Jim's friend, Luz. Write *Yes* or *No* in the boxes.

b What are three good presents for Luz?

8 SPEAKING EXCHANGE Find a present for a friend.

Student A: Close your book. Think of a friend.

Student B: Look at the chart on page 112. Ask questions to find a good present for Student A's friend. Then change roles.

Unit 6 Reference

Simple present

+		
I You	live work	in Chicago. near my brother. next to a bank.
He She It	live**s** work**s**	
We They	live work	

With *he*, *she*, and *it*, add *-s* to the verb.

–			
I You	don't	like eat	chicken. coffee. salad.
He She It	doesn't	like eat	
We They	don't	like eat	

?			
Do	I you	design write	books?
Does	he she it	design write	
Do	we they	design write	

Yes, I/you/we/they do.
Yes, he/she/it does.

No, I/you/we/they don't.
No, he/she/it doesn't.

?
What do you design?
Where do you live?
Who do you like?

For verbs ending in *-ch*, *-sh*, *-ss*, and *-o*, add *-es* to the verb with *he*, *she*, and *it*: *He/She/It watch**es***

I You We They	eat breakfast. go to work. finish work early. watch TV.
He She It	eat**s** breakfast. go**es** to work. finish**es** work early. watch**es** TV.

Object pronouns

Object pronouns are the object of a verb. They come after the verb.

Subject pronouns	Object pronouns
I/you/he/she/it/we/they	*me/you/him/her/it/us/them*

*Do you like **me**?* *I like **you**.* *We like **him**.*
*He likes **her**.* *She likes **it**.* *They like **us**.*
*I like **them**.*

Unit Vocabulary

Adjectives
tall ugly poor happy young
sad rich heavy intelligent
old thin short good-looking

Jobs and activities
architects design buildings
construction workers build buildings
fashion designers design clothes
reporters write articles chefs cook food
sales reps sell things

Daily activities
get up eat breakfast start work
go to bed take a shower finish work
watch TV eat a salad

Use *not very* to make negative descriptions more polite:

*She's **not very** intelligent.*
*They're **not very** rich.*

UNIT 7

A day at work

A

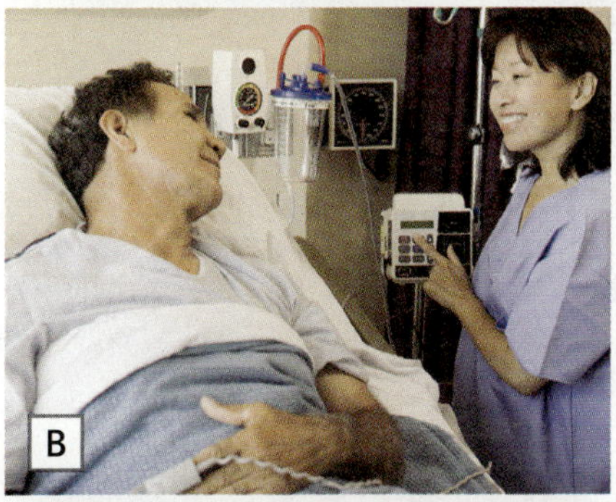

B

C

D

Warm Up

1 Match each photo or picture to a word in the box.

____ office	____ store	____ factory	____ restaurant
____ lab	____ school	____ hospital	____ university

E

F

G

H

2a Match an occupation to a photo or picture.

____ 1. a waiter
____ 2. an office worker
____ 3. a factory worker
____ 4. a nurse
____ 5. a sales clerk
____ 6. a professor
____ 7. a researcher
____ 8. a teacher

b 2.10 Listen and check your answers.

LESSON 1

Understand simple instructions

GRAMMAR imperatives

Listening and Vocabulary

1a 2.11 Listen. Who are the people in the pictures? Where are they?

b Listen again. Write a conversation number next to each phrase below.

2 a. Please sit down. ____ d. Turn off your cell phone. ____ f. Look at page 32.

____ b. Hold on, please. ____ e. Listen to the conversation. ____ g. Come in.

____ c. Be quiet.

c Write an underlined phrase from Exercise 1b under its picture below.

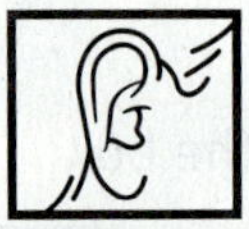
1. *listen to*

2. ____________

3. ____________

4. ____________

5. ____________

6. ____________

7. ____________

Grammar | imperatives

2 Write a phrase from Exercise 1b in the Active Grammar box.

3 Fill in the blanks with a word or phrase from the box.

Turn off	~~Don't be~~	Speak	Use	Don't text

1. *Don't be* late.
2. ____________ English in class.
3. ____________ your friends.
4. ____________ your cell phone.
5. ____________ a good dictionary.

Active Grammar

+ *Be quiet.*
  ____________ *at page 45.*

– *Don't* ____________ *in.*
  Don't ____________ *down.*

Use *please* to make an imperative polite.

***Please** be quiet./Be quiet, **please**.*
***Please** don't look at my email./Don't look at my email, **please**.*

See Reference page 78

4 ▶2.12 Listen. Match each imperative to a place below.

____ a. hospital ____ b. store ____ c. airport __1__ d. restaurant ____ e. school

5 **Pair Work** What are ways to improve your English? Write imperatives.

Speak English every day.

Speaking

6a Read the How To box.

b **Group Work** Work in groups of three. Use the How To box to practice phone calls. Use the names below. Change roles each time.

1. Company = JK Designs
   A = Paul Walker B = Receptionist
   C = Ken Noda
2. Company = Budget Construction
   A = Angelo Romano B = Receptionist
   C = Sally Wood
3. Company = Renzo Rogers Architects
   A = Helen Davis B = Receptionist
   C = Eduardo Medina

How To:

Make a business phone call

Use *My name's* with people you don't know.
Use *It's* with people you know.

B: *Hello. Parkside School.*
A: *Can I speak to Mrs. Fisher, please?*
B: *Hold on, please.*
C: *Hello. Alice Fisher.*
A: *Hello, Mrs. Fisher. My name's Jake Parker./It's Jake.*

Reading

7 Read the article. Answer the questions.

1. What time does Tim start work?
2. What does Tim do between 8 A.M. and 9 A.M.?
3. Where does Tim have lunch?
4. What does Tim do between 3:30 P.M. and 6 P.M.?
5. What time does Tim finish work?
6. When does Tim have a long vacation?

Tim Clark—a teacher in the US

I start work at 8:00. I check homework and prepare lessons. I teach from 9:00 to 12:30. I eat lunch in my classroom—a sandwich or a salad.

In the afternoon, I teach from 1:30 to 3:30. After school, I teach football or I work in my classroom. I go home at 6:00 and I eat dinner. After dinner, I check homework and prepare lessons. I finish work at 9:30. Teachers work a lot, but we have a long vacation in July* and August.

* for help with months, look at Exercise 8a

Vocabulary | months

8a ▶2.13 Listen and read the months. Then listen and repeat.

January	February	March	April	May	June
July	August	September	October	November	December

b Look at the pictures of New York City on page 110 in the Speaking Exchange. Guess the month.

c **Pair Work** Complete the sentences with months. Explain.

1. My favorite month is . . . 2. I don't like . . .

My favorite month is June. It's warm, but it's not very hot.

Say how often you do something

CAN DO

GRAMMAR adverbs of frequency

Vocabulary | work phrases

1a **Group Work** What jobs (occupations) can you remember? Write a list.

b Look at the work phrases in the box. Match each picture to a phrase in the box.

___ attend meetings	___ write reports	___ give presentations	___ call customers
_1_ travel for work	___ help people	___ answer the phone	___ work outdoors

1

2

3

4

5

6

7

8
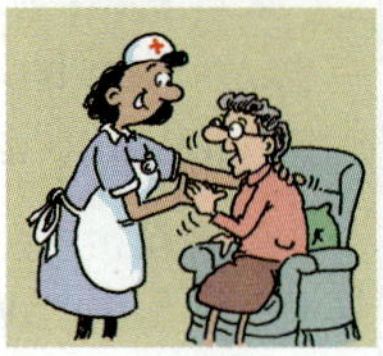

Listening

2a ▶ 2.14 Listen to the *What's your job?* game. Check (✓) Yes or No in the chart below.

b Listen again. Complete the conversation with the words or phrases in the box.

always (x2)	usually	not often
often (x2)	never	sometimes (x2)

WHAT'S YOUR JOB?

	Yes	No
attend meetings	✓	___
give presentations	___	___
call customers	___	___
write reports	___	___
travel for work	___	___
answer the phone	___	___
work outdoors	___	___
help people	___	___

H: Hi, John. Are you ready?
J: Yes, I'm _always_ (1.) ready!
H: OK, let's start. Do you attend meetings?
J: Yes, I ___________ (2.) attend meetings.
H: Do you give presentations?
J: Yes, I ___________ (3.) give presentations.
H: Do you call customers?
J: Yes, I ___________ (4.) call customers.
H: Do you write reports?
J: Yes, I do, but I ___________ (5.) write reports.
H: Do you travel for work?
J: Yes, I ___________ (6.) travel for work.
H: Do you answer the phone?
J: Yes, I ___________ (7.) answer the phone.
H: Do you work outside?
J: No, I ___________ (8.) work outside.
H: Do you help people?
J: Yes, I ___________ (9.) help people.
H: Are you a . . . sales rep?
J: Yes, I am!

Grammar | adverbs of frequency

3 Look at the conversation in Exercise 2b again. Complete the Active Grammar box.

4 **Pair Work** Take turns making sentences about your daily routines. Use a phrase from the box and an adverb of frequency.

get up	go to bed	start work
watch TV	finish work	take a shower
eat (something for) breakfast/lunch/dinner		

I usually get up at seven o'clock.

Active Grammar

100% always
usually
often
sometimes
not often/not usually
0% never

1. verb *be* + adverb of frequency
   I' ____ __________ *ready!*
2. adverb of frequency + verb
   I __________ *attend meetings.*
   I don't often write reports.

See Reference page 78

Pronunciation | word stress

5a 2.15 Listen. Mark the stress.

1. <u>al</u>ways 2. usually 3. often 4. sometimes 5. never

b Listen again. Then repeat.

Speaking

6 **Pair Work** Take turns asking and answering questions about jobs.

Student A: Choose a job (or use your own).

Student B: Ask questions. Guess Student A's job.

Do you write reports?

Yes, I sometimes write reports.

Writing

7 Read the notes and the How To box. Then write a request to Benita.

1.
Hi Uma,
Can you answer my phone this afternoon? There is a meeting at two o'clock.
Thanks,
Guy

2.
Anna,
I'm at home today. Can you call me? I have some questions for you.
Many thanks,
Emi

How To:

Write a request note

Start: *(Hello/Hi) Jay,*
Request: *Can you (please) + [request]?*
Finish: *Thanks,/Many thanks, + [your name].*

Hello Benita,

LESSON 3 Welcome a visitor to your place of work

CAN DO

GRAMMAR *would like:* preferences and offers

Listening

1a **Pair Work** Take turns saying the months of the year.

January *February* *March*

b 2.16 Listen and write on the calendar:

1. today 2. Mr. Wu 3. Mrs. King 4. Ms. Brown 5. Mr. Rodriguez

Vocabulary | ordinal numbers

2a 2.17 Look at the calendar again. Listen and repeat the ordinal numbers.

b **Pair Work** Look at the calendar above. Take turns saying the ordinal numbers.

3 Read the How To box.

4 **Pair Work** Stand and talk to your classmates. Ask and answer about birthdays.

When is your birthday? *It's on . . .*

How To:

Write and say dates

Say *-th* after the number (except for *first*, *second*, and *third*).

Write	Say
September 1 / 9.1	*September first*
July 2 / 7.2	*July second*
April 3 / 4.3	*April third*
January 15 / 1.15	*January fifteenth*

See Reference page 78

Grammar | *would like:* preferences and offers

5a ▶2.18 Read and listen to the conversation. Fill in the blanks.

Michelle: Please come in. Have a seat. What would you like _to_ (1.) drink? Tea? Coffee?
Mr. Rodriguez: I'd like coffee.
Ms. Khan: I'd ____________ (2.) a cup of tea, please.
Michelle: Would you like milk or sugar?
Mr. Rodriguez: No, thank you.
Ms. Khan: Milk, no sugar, please.

b **Group Work** Practice the conversation in groups of three. Change roles.

6 Complete the Active Grammar box with *would* or *'d*.

Active Grammar

Would you like . . . ? and *I'd like . . .* are polite.
Do you want . . . ? and *I want . . .* are informal.

would like + noun

?	*What would you like (to drink/to eat)?*	
	______ you like coffee?	
	Yes, please.	*No, thank you.*
+	*I______ like*	*coffee.*
	('d = would)	*a cup of coffee.*

See Reference page 78

Speaking

7 **Pair Work** Practice welcoming visitors.

Student A: You are a visitor. **Student B:** Welcome Student A. Offer drinks and snacks.

Hello, Mrs. Lee. My name is Pedro García.
Nice to meet you, Mr. García.
Please, come in.

Vocabulary | food and drink

8 Match the words in the box to the pictures below.

____ soup	____ desserts
____ fruit	____ appetizers
____ salad	____ vegetables
____ drinks	____ main courses
____ snacks	

Listening

9 ▶2.19 Listen to Michelle, Mr. Rodriguez, and Ms. Khan. Fill in the blanks on the map of the company cafeteria.

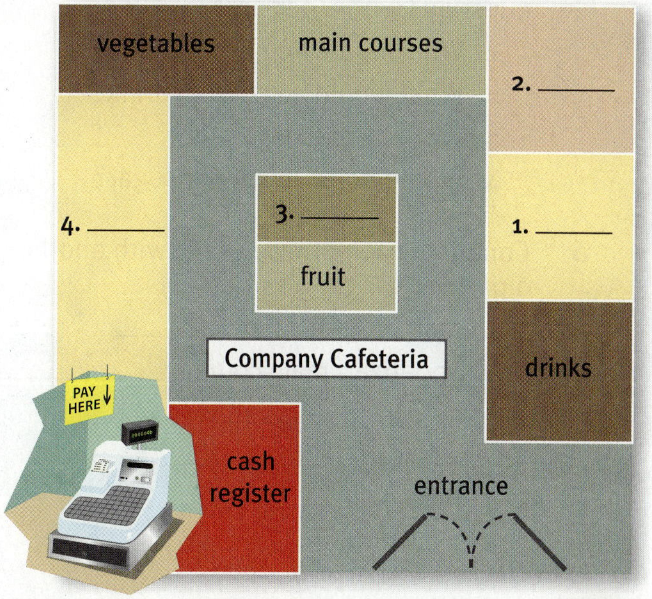

Extra Listening Activity in ACTIVEBOOK

Review

1 Use the words to write imperatives.

1. down/Please/sit
   Please sit down.
2. your/phone/cell/Turn off
   ______
3. late/don't/Please/be
   ______
4. at/look/50/page/Please
   ______

2 Circle the correct word.

1. They don't *sometimes/often/never* give presentations.
2. I *sometimes/never/usually* get up late. I get up at 6 o'clock every day.
3. He *never/doesn't usually/often* works late. He's a manager and he has a lot of work.
4. Tom and Kevin are good sales reps. They *always/never/sometimes* listen to their customers.

3 Use the word in parentheses to write a sentence.

1. Francis helps people. (always)
   Francis always helps people.
2. I attend meetings on Mondays. (sometimes)
   ______
3. She doesn't watch TV in the evening. (usually)
   ______
4. He is late for work. (never)
   ______
5. You aren't home in the evening. (usually)
   ______
6. We don't write reports. (often)
   ______

4 Match each question to a reply. Then practice asking and answering the questions with a partner.

1. What would you like to eat?
2. What would you like to drink?
3. Would you like coffee?
4. Would you like milk or sugar?

a. I'd like bottled water, please.
b. I'd like a salad, please.
c. Milk, no sugar, please.
d. Yes, please.

5 Complete each phrase or list with another word. Then share your answers with a partner.

1. March, April, *May*
2. appetizer, main course, ______
3. hold ______
4. a factory ______
5. June, July, ______
6. answer the ______
7. milk or ______
8. September, October, ______
9. a student, a teacher, ______
10. a fashion ______
11. fifth, sixth, ______
12. nineteenth, twentieth, ______

Communication | get and give directions in a building

6 **Pair Work** Talk about the different floors of the building.

What floor are the sales reps on?

They're on the fourth floor.

3rd Floor

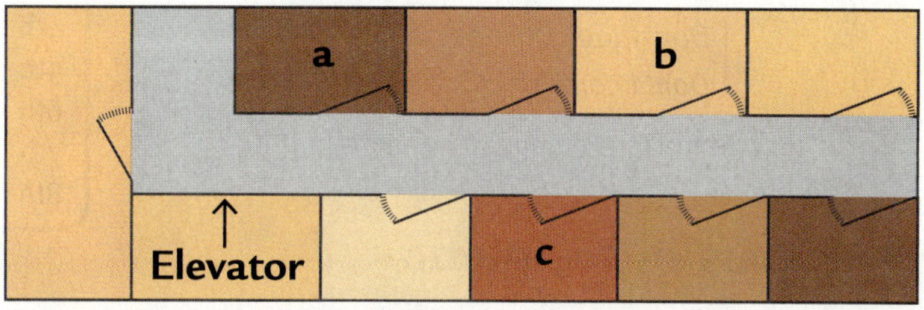

7a Who says the phrases below, the receptionist (*R*) or the visitor (*V*)?

____ 1. I'm here to see . . .
____ 2. Do you have an appointment?
____ 3. What's your name, please?
____ 4. How do you spell that?
____ 5. Take the elevator to the third floor.
____ 6. Thank you.
____ 7. You're welcome.

b 2.20 Listen and check your answers.

8 Listen again. Match the places below to the letters on the floor plan.

____ 1. Martina Hafner's office
____ 2. Lorda Romero's office
____ 3. Patrick Swinton's office

9 **Pair Work** Practice giving directions in a building. Change roles.

Student A: You are the receptionist. Think of the name of someone who works in the building. Write it on the floor plan. Tell your partner the name.

Student B: You are a visitor. Listen to the name Student A tells you. You have a meeting with this person. Act out the conversation.

Good morning.

Good morning. I have a meeting with . . .

Unit 7 Reference

Imperatives

⊕	*Be quiet.*
	Sit down.
⊖	*Don't talk.*
	Don't sit down.

Affirmative imperatives

(Please) *Sit down.*
Turn off your cell phone.
Look at page 32.
Come in.

Negative imperatives

(Please) *Don't sit down.*
Don't turn off your cell phone.
Don't look at page 32.
Don't come in.

Use *please* to make the imperative more polite.

Adverbs of frequency

100%	always
	usually
	often
	sometimes
	not often/not usually
0%	never

Adverbs of frequency come **after** the verb *be*.

*She's **always** late.*
*They're **never** happy.*

Adverbs of frequency come **before** other verbs.

*He **doesn't often** give presentations.*
*We **don't usually** eat desserts.*

Would you like . . .? I'd like . . .

Use *would like* to offer food or drink to guests.

*What **would** you **like**?*
*What **would** you **like** to drink?*
***Would** you **like** coffee?*
Yes, please./No, thank you.

Use *I'd like* . . . to say what you prefer.

***I'd like** a cup of tea, please.*
***I'd like** an appetizer, please.*

Ordinal numbers

Add *-th* to make most ordinal numbers (except for first, second, and third).

1st	first	9th	ninth	17th	seventeenth
2nd	second	10th	tenth	18th	eighteenth
3rd	third	11th	eleventh	19th	nineteenth
4th	fourth	12th	twelfth	20th	twentieth
5th	fifth	13th	thirteenth	21st	twenty-first
6th	sixth	14th	fourteenth	22nd	twenty-second
7th	seventh	15th	fifteenth		
8th	eighth	16th	sixteenth		

Dates

Writing dates		Saying dates
August 21	*8.21*	*August twenty-first*

Unit Vocabulary

Work places

office, factory, hospital, university, store, school, cafeteria, lab

Months

January, April, July, October, February, May, August, November, March, June, September, December

Work phrases

attend meetings, give presentations, work outdoors, call customers, write reports, travel for work, answer the phone

Food

fruit, soup, appetizers, desserts, drinks, salad, vegetables, snacks, main courses

UNIT 8
Your likes and dislikes

Warm Up

1a Match each leisure activity in the box to its picture below.

go biking	go out to eat	play chess	go hiking	play tennis	go sightseeing
work out	read a book	play soccer	watch TV	go swimming	~~go to the theater~~

1.  *go to the theater*
2.  ________
3.  ________
4.  ________
5.  ________
6.  ________
7.  ________
8.  ________
9.  ________
10.  ________
11.  ________
12.  ________

b 2.21 Listen and check. Then repeat.

2 **Pair Work** How often do you do these activities? Tell your partner.

LESSON 1

Explain why you want to do something

CAN DO

GRAMMAR *like* + gerund/infinitive; *want* + infinitive

Speaking

1a Look at the destinations. What can you see in the photos?

b Read the How To box. What activities can you do at each destination?

2 **Group Work** What's a nice place you like to visit? What can you do there?

> **How To:**
>
> **Talk about things to do**
>
> Use *You can* . . . or *We can* . . . to talk about things to do in a place.
>
> *You can play golf in Palm Springs.*
>
> *We can go sightseeing in San Francisco.*

Listening

3a 2.22 Listen. What is Gary and Annie's problem?

b 2.23 Listen. Complete the sentences.

1. Gary wants to go to __________.
2. Annie wants to go to __________.
3. They both want to go to __________.

Pronunciation | reduction of sounds: *want to*

4a 2.24 Listen. How is *want to* pronounced in these sentences?

b Listen again. Then repeat.

Grammar | *like* + gerund/infinitive; *want* + infinitive

5 Complete the Active Grammar box with *want* or *like*. Check Audioscript 2.23 on page 122 for help.

Active Grammar

⊕ *I ____________ playing (or to play) golf.*	⊕ *I ____________ to go sightseeing.*
⊖ *I don't like going (or to go) sightseeing.*	⊖ *I don't want to play golf.*

See Reference page 88

6 Circle the correct forms of the verb to complete the sentences.

1. I like *going out/to go out* with friends.
2. Gary doesn't want *watching/to watch* TV.
3. Do you want *playing/to play* tennis?
4. We like *going/to go* sightseeing.
5. She doesn't want *going out/to go out* to eat.
6. Do they like *playing/to play* chess?
7. I don't like *swimming/to go swimming*.
8. Martin wants *reading/to read* now.

Vocabulary | adjectives

7 Match each word in the box to its situation below.

boring	~~exciting~~	fun
difficult	interesting	easy

1\. 

This is really *exciting*.

3\. 

This is ____________.

5\. 

This is very ____________.

2\. 

This is very ____________.

4\. 

This is ____________.

6\. 

This is really ____________.

Speaking

8 **Group Work** Choose a destination from Exercise 1a for next weekend. Stand and find other students to go with you.

Writing

9 Look at the Writing Bank on page 117. Then write an email to a hotel in one of the destinations in Exercise 1a.

LESSON 2 Say what things you possess

CAN DO

GRAMMAR *have/has*

Vocabulary | rooms and furniture

1a **Pair Work** Look at the house. Ask and answer questions. Where do you:

a. cook? b. watch TV? c. take a shower? d. go to bed? e. park your car? f. play soccer?

Where do you cook? *I cook in the kitchen.*

b Match the words in the box to the items in the picture.

J dishwasher	___ sofa	___ bed	___ bicycle	___ bathtub	___ wardrobe
___ coffee table	___ lamp	___ car	___ cabinet	___ window	___ armchair
___ mirror	___ toilet	___ sink	___ fridge	___ stove	

American English	British English
stove	*cooker*

c 2.25 Listen and check your answers. Then listen and repeat.

Listening

2a 2.26 Listen. Which items from Exercise 1b do you hear? Circle them.

b Listen again. Put a check (✓) next to the things in Exercise 1b that Pablo's sister has.

c Look at Jo's suggestion for a wedding present on page 110 in the Speaking Exchange. Do you think it's a good idea? Why or why not?

Grammar | *have/has*

3a Look at Audioscript 2.26 on pages 122–123. Underline examples of *have* and *has*.

b Complete the Active Grammar box with *have, has, do,* or *does.*

Active Grammar

I / *You* / *We* / *They*	⊕	______	*a bicycle.* / *a sofa.* / *a yard.* / *a garage.*
	⊖	*don't* ______	
He / *She* / *It*	⊕	______	
	⊖	*doesn't* ______	
?	______	*I/you/we/they have*	*a bicycle?*
?	______	*he/she/it have*	*an armchair?*

Yes, I/you/we/they ______. *Yes, he/she/it* ______.
No, I/you/we/they ______. *No, he/she/it* ______.

See Reference page 88

4 **Pair Work** Ask your partner questions with the words in Exercise 1b.

Do you have any armchairs?

Yes, I do. I have two armchairs in my living room, and I have one armchair in my bedroom.

Speaking

5 **Pair Work** Find a new partner. Talk about your house, apartment, or bedroom.

My family has an apartment. It's pretty big. I have a small bedroom. I have a TV and a computer in my bedroom, but I don't have . . .

Reading

6 **SPEAKING EXCHANGE** Do the *Technology* quiz on page 112. Ask your partner the questions and write his or her answers.

Do you have an e-book reader?

No, I don't, but I want one.

7a Add your points and find your score.

b **Pair Work** Read your score results. Are the score results true? Discuss with your partner.

A = 2 points   B = 1 point   C = 0 points

0–6 points: You don't like new technology; you like old things. Your photographs are on paper, not on your computer. You use a map—you don't use a GPS device. Your television is quite old. You don't like to spend money on new technology.

7–12 points: You like new technology and you sometimes buy new things. You sometimes read about new technology in newspapers and magazines. You take a lot of digital photos.

13–18 points: You really like new technology. You have the newest cell phone. You often read about new technology in newspapers and magazines. You like to spend money on new technology.

LESSON 3

Suggest a restaurant; make reservations; order food

CAN DO

GRAMMAR *wh-* question words: *which/how*

Listening

1a 2.27 Listen to Mark and Anna. Which restaurant do they want to go to?

____ a. Sinatra's ____ b. Wasabi ____ c. Carlito's

b Listen again. Number the questions in the order you hear them.

____ Where's that?
____ What kind of food do they serve?
1 How about dinner next Friday?
____ How big is it?
____ What about Carlito's?
____ Which restaurant do you want to go to?

2 **Group Work** Read the How To box. In groups of four, suggest local restaurants for tonight.

How To:

Make suggestions

What about dinner next week?	*Good idea!/Yes./OK.*
How about Luciano's Restaurant?	*No, I don't like that restaurant.*

Grammar | question words

3 Match the questions in the Active Grammar box to the answers below.

____ a. He likes all kinds of food.
____ b. It's near my house.
____ c. She's a chef.
____ d. It's very big.
____ e. I like the new one.
____ f. He's my friend.

Active Grammar

Where	1. *Where is Carlito's?*
Who	2. *Who is he?*
What	3. *What does she do?*
What kind of + noun	4. *What kind of food does he like?*
Which + noun	5. *Which restaurant do you like—the new one or the old one?*
How + adjective	6. *How big is it?*

See Reference page 88

4 Complete the sentences with question words from the Active Grammar box.

1. *How* rich is she?
2. ____________ fruit do you like?
3. ____________ do you live?
4. ____________ is your boss?
5. ____________ 's your name?
6. ____________ sofa do you like—this one or that one?

Speaking

5 **Pair Work** Read the How To box. Make reservations.

Student A: Call Carlito's restaurant. Reserve a table for Saturday evening.

Student B: You work at Carlito's restaurant. Answer the phone.

How To:

Reserve a table at a restaurant

Customer:	*I'd like to reserve a table for Friday afternoon/Saturday night.*
Waiter:	*How many people?* *What time?* *What's the name, please?*

Vocabulary | food

6a Match the underlined words in the menu to the pictures.

1. *chicken*
2. ______
3. ______
4. ______
5. ______
6. ______
7. ______
8. ______
9. ______
10. ______

b 2.28 Listen and check your answers.

c **Pair Work** Say what food you like or don't like from the menu.

d **Group Work** Choose your favorite appetizer, main course, and dessert from the menu. Tell the group.

I'd like the fish soup, the lamb chops for the main course, and the ice cream for dessert.

7a 2.29 Listen. What do Mark and Anna choose from the menu?

b **Group Work** Work in groups of three. Look at Audioscript 2.29 on page 123. Read the conversation aloud but change the food.

Are you ready to order?

Yes. I'd like a house salad, please.

Speaking

8 **SPEAKING EXCHANGE** Work in groups of three.

Student A: You are the waiter at Salt and Pepper restaurant.

Students B and C: You are customers at Salt and Pepper restaurant. Look at the menu on page 109. Enter the restaurant and order your meal.

Good evening. Do you have a reservation?

Yes, we do. My name is . . .

Extra Listening Activity in ACTIVEBOOK

Review

1 Complete the conversation with the correct form of the words in parentheses. Then practice with a partner.

A: Do you want *to go* (1. go) to a movie this afternoon?
B: There's a good movie on TV. Do you want ______ (2. watch) TV?
A: I don't like ______ (3. watch) TV.
B: OK. Well, I like ______ (4. swim), and it's hot today. Do you want ______ (5. go) swimming?
A: I can't swim. Do you want ______ (6. go) sightseeing?
B: Yes. I want ______ (7. take) some photos with my new camera.

2 Complete the email with the correct form of *have*.

> Hi Benita,
>
> Thanks for your email. Please come to my house when you visit Vancouver. *I have* (1. I/✓) a guest bedroom, so you can stay there. ______ (2. it/✓) a big bed and an armchair. ______ (3. it/✗) a television, but ______ (4. it/✓) a bathroom. Can you drive? ______ (5. I/✗) a car, but ______ (6. my parents/✓) one. ______ (7. you) a bicycle? ______ (8. My husband/✓) one, and you can use it.
>
> See you next week!
>
> Love,
>
> Amy

3 Write questions and answers using *have* and the words in parentheses. Then practice with a partner.

1. A: *Does your sister have a dishwasher*? (your sister/dishwasher)
   B: *Yes, she does*. (Yes)
2. A: ______? (you/car)
   B: ______. (No)
3. A: ______? (your parents/TV)
   B: ______. (No)
4. A: ______? (James/bicycle)
   B: ______. (Yes)
5. A: ______? (they/new email address)
   B: ______. (No)
6. A: ______? (she/good dictionary)
   B: ______. (Yes)

4 Write a question for each answer. Use *what*, *where*, *who*, *how*, *which*, or *what kind of*. Then practice with a partner.

1. A: *What do you do*?
   B: I'm a teacher.
2. A: ______?
   B: She's not very tall.
3. A: ______?
   B: I like Italian food and Chinese food.
4. A: ______?
   B: I like this coffee table. That coffee table is small.
5. A: ______?
   B: I live in Quito in Ecuador.
6. A: ______?
   B: She's my friend.

Communication | ask for and give information about people

5 **Pair Work** Look at the people and their apartments. What does each person like doing? Tell your partner.

9c: He likes playing golf.

9b: She likes to watch sports.

6 **Pair Work** Complete four of the addresses below. Don't show your partner.

Student A: Look at page 110 in the Speaking Exchange.
Student B: Look at page 111 in the Speaking Exchange.

Mr. O. Pamuk 7 Oak Lane ______	Ms. A. Walker 7 Oak Lane ______	Mr. S. Kato 7 Oak Lane ______	Ms. T. Morrison 7 Oak Lane ______	Mr. J. Heller 7 Oak Lane ______
Ms. Z. Smith 7 Oak Lane ______	Mr. J. Coe 7 Oak Lane ______	Mr. M. Haddon 7 Oak Lane ______	Ms. M. Atwood 7 Oak Lane ______	Mrs. A. Garcia 7 Oak Lane ______

7 **Pair Work** Ask your partner *Yes/No* questions with *like* to complete the other four addresses.

Does Mr. Coe like reading?

No, he doesn't. Does Ms. Walker . . .

Unit 8 Reference

like + gerund/infinitive; *want* + infinitive

When a verb follows *like*, it is in the gerund form (*-ing*) or the infinitive form (*to* + verb).

*I like **reading**.* *I like **to read**.*

When a verb follows *want*, it is always in the infinitive form (*to* + verb).

*I want **to read**.*

have

Have is an irregular verb.

	I / You / We / They	(+) have (−) don't have		a bicycle. a televison. a brother. two sisters.
	He / She / It	(+) has (−) doesn't have		
?	Do	I/you/we/they	have	any cousins?
?	Does	he/she/it		a cat?

Yes, I/you/we/they do.
Yes, he/she/it does.
No, I/you/we/they don't.
No, he/she/it doesn't.

Question words

- Use *where* for places.
  ***Where** are you from?*
  ***Where** do you live?*
- Use *who* for people.
  ***Who** are you?*
  ***Who** do you play tennis with?*

You can also use *who* to ask about the company someone works for.

***Who** do you work for?*

- Use *what* for things.
  ***What**'s your name?*
  ***What** do you do?*
- Use *what kind of* + noun for types.
  ***What kind of** ice cream is there?*
  ***What kind of** books do you have?*
- Use *which* for things when there is a choice.
  ***Which** dictionary do you have?*
  ***Which** John Lennon song is your favorite?*
- Use *how* + adjective for amounts.
  ***How** tall is he?*
  ***How** old are you?*
- Note these questions:
  How much is it? (price)
  How many cars do you have? (quantity)
  How often do you go out? (frequency)

Make suggestions

Use *What about . . . ?* or *How about . . .?* + noun to make suggestions.

***What about** the new restaurant on Clark Street?*
***How about** a week at the beach this summer?*

Unit Vocabulary

Leisure activities

go biking, go hiking, play tennis, watch TV, play chess, go sightseeing, go out to eat, read a book, go swimming, go to the theater, play soccer, work out

Adjectives

boring, easy, exciting, difficult, fun, interesting

Rooms and furniture

living room:	sofa	coffee table	
	lamp	armchair	
bedroom:	bed	window	wardrobe
kitchen:	sink	fridge	dishwasher
	stove	cabinet	
bathroom:	sink	mirror	
	toilet	bathtub	
garage:	car	bicycle	

Food

fish, rice, beef, lamb, pasta, cheese, potatoes, seafood, chicken, chocolate

UNIT 9
Your life

A Beijing Summer Olympics

B Wall Street Crash

C Fall of the Berlin Wall

D Mandela: New President of South Africa

Warm Up

1 Look at the photos. Match each photo to a year. ____ 1989 ____ 1994 ____ 2008 ____ 1929

2a Match a year in the box to a headline below.

1963	1946	2011	1977	2004	1912	2002	2010

____ a. First iPod in Stores
____ b. William and Kate Royal Wedding
____ c. Tsunami in Southeast Asia
____ d. Titanic Disaster
____ e. Martin Luther King: "I have a dream"
____ f. Haiti Earthquake
____ g. Juan Peron: President of Argentina
____ h. Elvis Presley Is Dead

b **Pair Work** Tell your partner what you think.

c 2.30 Listen and check your answers.

I think "First iPod in Stores" is 2004.

I think it's 2002.

LESSON 1

Make simple statements about people from history

CAN DO

GRAMMAR simple past of *be:* affirmative statements

A Michael Jackson

B Princess Diana

C Elvis Presley

D Bruce Lee

Reading

1a Read the biographies. Match a biography to a photo.

____ 1. He was a singer and an actor. He was born on January 8, 1935. His parents were very poor. He was a factory worker and then a truck driver. His first song was "That's All Right." He was "The King of Rock and Roll."

____ 2. He was a singer and dancer. He was born on August 29, 1958. He was the lead singer of a group at the age of 11. His album *Thriller* was the top album of all time. He was "The King of Pop."

____ 3. He was an actor and fighter. He was born on November 27, 1940, in San Francisco. His parents were from Hong Kong. They weren't rich. His father was a singer. His last movie was *Enter the Dragon.* He was short and thin, but he was very strong and fast.

____ 4. She was a princess and a fashion icon. She was born on July 1, 1961. Her parents were rich. She wasn't a good student at school, but she was a good pianist. Her husband was Prince Charles. Their life together was not happy.

b Complete the sentences with names from the photos.

1. *Michael Jackson* and *Elvis Presley* were singers.
2. ____________ and ____________ were actors.
3. ____________ and ____________ were poor as children.
4. ____________ was rich.

c **Pair Work** Close your books. What can you remember about the people in the paragraphs in Exercise 1a?

Bruce Lee was born in San Francisco. His parents were . . .

Grammar | simple past of *be*: affirmative statements

2a Complete the Active Grammar box with *was* or *were*.

b 2.31 Listen and check your answers.

Active Grammar

I	*was*	*an actor.*
You	*were*	*a singer.*
He	______	*happy.*
She	______	*born in 1982.*
It	______	*great.*
We	*were*	*singers.*
They	______	*rich.*

See Reference page 98

3 Complete the sentences with *was* or *were*.

1. Coco Chanel *was* a fashion designer.
2. Picasso and Matisse ______ famous for their paintings.
3. Colonel Tom Parker ______ Elvis Presley's manager.
4. Jackie Chan and Oprah Winfrey ______ born in 1954.
5. We ______ good soccer players in 1990. We don't play soccer now.
6. I ______ a good pianist at school.

4a Read the How To box. Then write two true sentences and one false sentence about you and your family.

How To:
Talk about childhood

When I was a child, I was a good singer.
When they were young, they were very poor.

b **Pair Work** Read your sentences to your partner. Your partner guesses true or false.

When my father was young, he was an actor.

False.

No, it's true!

Vocabulary | collocations with prepositions

5a Complete the biographies with prepositions from the box.

on for with ~~in~~ of at

She was <u>born</u> *in* (1.) 1929 in New York. She was <u>good</u> ______ (2.) horseback-riding and painting. Her husbands were John F. Kennedy, the <u>president</u> ______ (3.) the US, and then Aristotle Onassis, a Greek businessman.

Billie Holiday was <u>born</u> ______ (4.) April 7, 1915, in Philadelphia. She was <u>famous</u> ______ (5.) her music. She was <u>friends</u> ______ (6.) the jazz musician Lester Young. Her husbands were bad men and she was unhappy.

b **Pair Work** Say an underlined word from the paragraphs above. Your partner says the preposition.

good

good at

6a Who is your favorite person from the 20th century? Write notes about him or her.

b **Pair Work** Tell your partner about this person. Your partner guesses the person.

He was born in the UK. He was a singer and songwriter.

Give a short description of a past experience

GRAMMAR simple past of *be*: negatives and questions

CAN DO

Poker

Scrabble

Mahjong

Speaking

1 **Pair Work** Talk about the games. Use the phrases below.

I know how to play . . . | *I don't know how to play . . .* | *It's difficult/easy/boring/ exciting/fun/interesting.*

Listening

2a 2.32 Listen to Kenji, Isabella, and Mei Ling playing a game called *my first, my last*. In the game you can't answer questions with *yes* or *no*. What does Isabella talk about?

b Listen again. Circle the correct words about Kenji and Mei Ling below.

KENJI'S FIRST TEACHER

1. Her name was *Miss/Mrs.* Lloyd.
2. She was about *50/60* years old.
3. She was a *good/bad* teacher.
4. Her favorite student was *Koji/Kenji*.

MEI LING'S LAST VACATION

1. Mei Ling's last vacation was *two/three* years ago.
2. It was to a *Pacific/Caribbean* island.
3. Mei Ling was with *her parents/a friend*.
4. There were *mountains/beaches* on the island.

Grammar | simple past of *be*: negatives and questions

3 Look at Audioscript 2.32 on page 123 and complete the Active Grammar box with *was*, *wasn't*, or *were*.

Active Grammar

−	*I _______ (was not)*	*a good student.*	? *Was I*	*a good student?*
	You weren't	*happy at school.*	*_______ you*	*happy at school?*
	He/She/It _______	*interesting.*	*_______ he/she/it*	*interesting?*
	We weren't	*good students.*	*Were we*	*good students?*
	They weren't	*in my class.*	*Were they*	*in my class?*

? *What was her name?* *Who was your favorite teacher?*
Where were your books? *When was your class?*

See Reference page 98

Chess

Monopoly

4 Complete the sentences with *was*, *wasn't*, *were*, or *weren't*.

1. I *was* ______ very quiet at school. (✓)
2. My first car ______ very big, but it was fun. (✗)
3. Who ______ your friends at school?
4. What ______ your favorite subject at school?
5. You ______ at school. (✗)
6. ______ you late this morning?

Pronunciation | sentence stress

5 ▶2.33 Listen. Mark the stress.

1. I was a good student.
2. He wasn't very intelligent.
3. They weren't very happy.
4. Was she a good teacher?
5. Who were your friends?

Vocabulary | time expressions: *yesterday, last, ago*

6 Complete the time expressions with *yesterday, ago,* or *last*.

1. today
2. yesterday
3. ______ night
4. ______ morning
5. two days ______
6. ______ week
7. ______ month
8. six months ______
9. ______ year
10. ten years ______

Speaking

7a **Pair Work** When were these past experiences? Tell your partner.

- your first day at school
- your last meal in a restaurant
- your first vacation
- your last flight
- your first job
- your first email

My first day at school was 22 years ago.

b **Pair Work** Ask your partner questions with *Where were you . . . ?* and a time expression.

Where were you yesterday afternoon?

I was at home.

8 SPEAKING EXCHANGE Work in groups of three or four. Play *my first, my last* on page 113.

Writing

9 Write a paragraph about your first teacher or your last vacation. You can start like this:

My first teacher was . . . She/He was . . .
My last vacation was (six months) ago . . . It was to . . .

LESSON 3

Make a simple request and ask permission

GRAMMAR *can/could I:* permission; *can/could you:* requests

CAN DO

Vocabulary | housework

1a Match a picture below to a phrase in the box.

_____ do the laundry	_____ vacuum the house	_____ cook dinner
_____ clean the bathroom	_____ wash the dishes	_____ iron a shirt

1 
2 
3 
4 
5 
6 

b 2.34 Listen and check your answers.

2 **Pair Work** Who does these things in your house? Tell your partner.

My wife does the laundry.

I iron my shirts.

Reading

3a Read the article.

Who does the housework now?

In the 1950s, life was simple. Women were housewives and men were factory workers, managers, sales reps, sales assistants, etc. But in the 21st century, life is different. Now, there are over 140,000 househusbands in the US. They stay at home and look after the children. We talk to one househusband, Jeff Timberland.

Do you like your job as a househusband?

Jeff: Yes, I do. Plus, childcare is $250 for one week, for one child. It's very expensive.

What does your wife do?

Jeff: She's an architect.

Do you like doing housework?

Jeff: I don't like ironing—it's very boring. And I don't like washing the dishes. But I like vacuuming the house and cooking dinner.

What was your job before?

Jeff: I was a sales rep. I was a good sales rep, and I was happy. But my children are my job now.

Do you want to get another job?

Jeff: Yes, but not now. My kids are very young. They want their dad, not a stranger.

b **Pair Work** Take turns asking and answering the questions below.

1. How many househusbands are there in the US now?
2. Does Jeff like his job as a househusband?
3. What is Jeff's wife's occupation?
4. What housework does Jeff like doing?
5. What did Jeff do before?
6. Does Jeff want to get a new job now?

c **Group Work** Work in small groups. Discuss.

1. Are there a lot of househusbands in your country?
2. Who usually looks after young children in your country?
3. Jeff says, "They want their dad, not a stranger." Do you agree?

Listening

4a 2.35 Listen to four events in Jeff's week. Match each conversation to its picture.

A 

B 

C 

D 

____ Conversation 1 ____ Conversation 2 ____ Conversation 3 ____ Conversation 4

b Listen again. Write the questions you hear beginning with *How was . . . ?*

1. How was ______________________?
2. How was ______________________?
3. How was ______________________?
4. How was ______________________?

5 **Group Work** Read the How To box. Work in small groups. Ask questions with *How was . . . ?*

How was your weekend?

It was fine, thanks. I went to a concert on Sunday

How To:

Ask about an experience

How was	*your weekend?/your week?/ your day?/your flight?*
It was great.	*It was OK.*
It wasn't very good.	*It was awful.*

Grammar | *Can/Could I . . . ?; Can/Could you . . . ?*

6 Complete the Active Grammar box with *I* or *you*.

Active Grammar

Can / *Could*	______	*use your telephone?* / *have a cup of coffee?*
Yes, ______ can.		*No, I'm sorry.*
Can / *Could*	______	*carry my bags?* / *iron my shirt?*
Yes, of course.		*I'm sorry, I can't.*

See Reference page 98

Speaking

7 **Pair Work** Use the cues to ask your partner questions.

- use your pen
- spell your name
- use your cell phone
- give me your email address
- give me some money
- open the window
- look at your book

Could I use your pen? *Yes, of course.*

Extra Listening Activity in ACTIVEBOOK

Review

1 Complete the paragraph with *was* or *were* and guess the famous person.

Who am I?

I am a singer with a very famous band. I _was_ (1.) born on July 26, 1943, in the UK. My father and my grandfather ________ (2.) teachers. My mother ________ (3.) from Australia. I ________ (4.) a student at the London School of Economics—but only for two years. Jerry Hall and Bianca Moreno de Macias ________ (5.) my wives. "Paint It Black" and "Satisfaction" ________ (6.) two of my band's famous songs.

2 Use the words to write sentences.

1. Sally/late/early _Sally wasn't late. She was early._
2. My parents/at home/at a restaurant _My parents weren't at home. They were at a restaurant._
3. Rick/born in 1981/born in 1979 ________
4. It/a good movie/very boring ________
5. We/rich/very poor ________
6. Kerry and Mark/in Bogotá/in Cali ________

3 Use the words to write questions. Match the questions with the answers below. Then ask and answer them with a partner.

1. born?/When/you/were _When were you born?_ = _e_
2. was/Who/manager?/your ________ = ____
3. school?/your/Where/was ________ = ____
4. first/What/your/job?/was ________ = ____
5. weekend?/your/was/How ________ = ____

a. I was a factory worker.
b. It was great, thanks.
c. Her name was Ms. Dickson.
d. It was on Peak Street, near the hospital.
e. In 1990.

4 Circle the correct word to complete each sentence.

1. Can *I/you* tell me the time?
2. Could *I/you* open the door?
3. Can *I/you* help you?
4. Can *I/you* tell me your name, please?
5. Could *I/you* pass me the salt, please?
6. Could *I/you* listen to your new CD?

5 Circle the correct word to complete each sentence.

1. Where were you *yesterday/last/ago* night?
2. Who usually *vacuums/cleans/does* the laundry?
3. I was in Colombia six months *yesterday/last/ago*.
4. What was she famous *on/to/for*?
5. Where were you *yesterday/last/ago* afternoon?
6. Can you *wash/vacuum/iron* the house today?
7. He's friends *of/with/to* Mark Heller.
8. Are you good *on/to/at* tennis?

Communication | talk about school days

6 ▶2.36 Match a subject in the box to a picture. Then listen and repeat.

____ math ____ languages ____ science ____ music ____ art ____ sports

American English	British English
math	maths
sports	sport

A

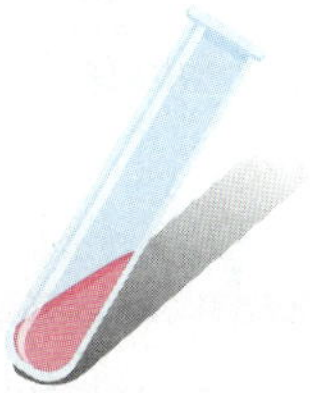

B

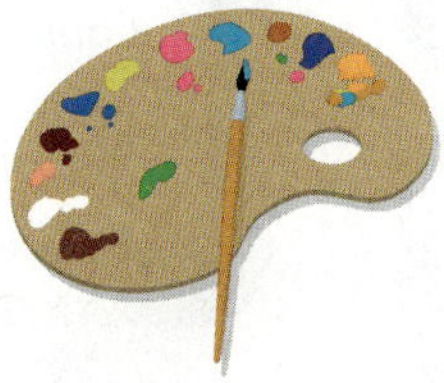

C $2(3x-11)=8 \quad y=?$

D

E

F Hello Bonjour Hola 你好

7a ▶2.37 Listen and complete the form for Louise.

b Listen again. Check your answers.

8a Complete the form in Exercise 7a so that it is true for you.

b **Pair Work** Make sentences based on the chart. Tell your partner.

My school days

School name: *Washington High School*	Good at: ______
	Bad at: ______
Where: ______	Favorite class: ______
Years: ______	Best friend: ______
Good/bad school	Good/bad student

I was very good at math.

Really? I wasn't. I was good at music.

9 **Group Work** Close your books and ask other students about their school days.

What was the name of your high school?

Were you a good student?

Unit 9 Reference

Simple past of *be*

+		
I	*was*	
You	*were*	*a teacher.*
He		*born in 1983.*
She	*was*	*very good.*
It		
We	*were*	*teachers.*
They	*were*	*born in 1983.*

–		
I	*wasn't (was not)*	
You	*weren't (were not)*	*a teacher.* *born in 1983.* *very good.*
He *She* *It*	*wasn't (was not)*	
We	*weren't (were not)*	*teachers.*
They	*weren't (were not)*	*born in 1983.*

?		
Was	*I*	
Were	*you*	*a teacher?*
	he	*born in 1983?*
Was	*she*	*very good?*
	it	
Were	*we*	*teachers?*
Were	*they*	*born in 1983?*

?
Who was your manager?
What were their names?
Where was your school?
Which store was your favorite?
When was the interview?
How old were you in 2000?

Asking permission

Can I *Could I*	*call you this evening?* *speak to Mrs. Walsh?* *use your computer?*

Yes, of course./Sure.
No, I'm sorry.

Use *Can I* and *Could I* to ask permission. *Can I* and *Could I* have the same meaning. *Could I* is a bit more polite/formal.

Making requests

Can you	*call me this evening?*
Could you	*answer the phone?*

Yes, of course./Sure.
No, I'm sorry.

Use *Can you* and *Could you* to make a request. *Can you* and *Could you* have the same meaning, but *Could you* is a bit more polite or formal.

Time expressions

Yesterday
yesterday yesterday evening yesterday afternoon yesterday morning

Last
last night last week last month last year

Ago
five months ago eight years ago two days ago a week ago

Unit Vocabulary

Adjectives and prepositions
born in (Paris) born on (October 3rd)
bad at (soccer) famous for (his books)
friends with (Madonna)
good at (tennis/dancing)
the president of the United States

Housework
do the laundry vacuum the house
cook dinner clean the bathroom
iron a shirt wash the dishes

UNIT 10
Past and future events

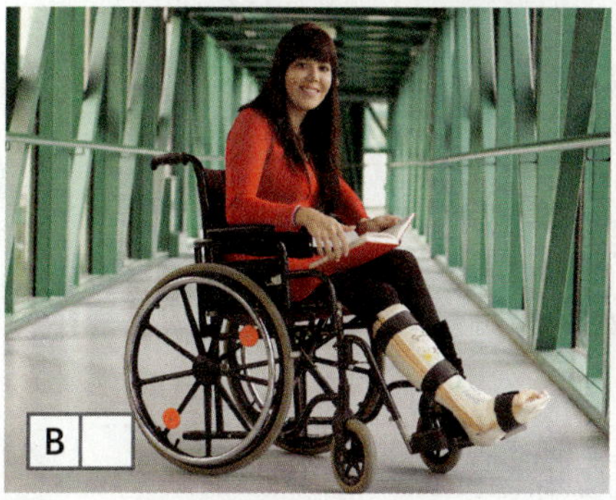

Warm Up

1a Complete each sentence with a verb from the box.

win	arrests	get	meet	~~lose~~	steals	find	break	stay	move

1. You *lose* ________ your wallet.
2. A thief ____________ your cell phone.
3. You ____________ in bed all day.
4. You ____________ the lottery.
5. You ____________ married.
6. You ____________ $10 on the street.
7. A police officer ____________ you.
8. You ____________ to a new house.
9. You ____________ your leg.
10. You ____________ your favorite actor.

b 2.38 Listen and check your answers.

c Look at the photos. Match each picture to a sentence in Exercise 1a.

Understand a simple narrative of past events

GRAMMAR simple past: regular verbs

The Story of the Mona Lisa (PART 1)

Every day, 15,000 people visit the Louvre museum in Paris. Most of them want to see the "Mona Lisa." But what is the story of this painting?

The artist was, of course, Leonardo da Vinci. He started the painting in 1503, and he finished it about four years later. Leonardo was Italian, but in 1516 he moved to France with the painting. The King of France liked it, and the "Mona Lisa" stayed in France.

Reading

1 Read "The Story of the Mona Lisa (Part 1)" aloud. Complete the information below.

Place (now): *The Louvre, Paris*

Artist: ______

Started painting: ______

Finished painting: ______

Moved to France: ______

Grammar | simple past affirmative: regular verbs

2a Underline the verbs in "The Story of the Mona Lisa (Part 1)."

b Which verbs are in the simple past?

c How do you make the simple past of regular verbs?

3 Complete the Active Grammar box with the correct form of the verb.

4 Complete each paragraph with verbs from each box in the simple past.

Active Grammar

simple present	simple past
I like the painting.	*I liked the painting.*
She stays with her friends.	*She ______ with her friends.*

See Reference page 108

finish ~~want~~ start ask

Pope Julius II *wanted* (1.) a new ceiling in the Sistine Chapel. He ______ (2.) Michelangelo to paint the ceiling of the Sistine Chapel. Michelangelo ______ (3.) it in 1508. He ______ (4.) it in 1512.

live work play move (x2)

Marcel Duchamp was an artist. He was born in 1887. He ______ (5.) in Paris, and he ______ (6.) chess with his brothers. In 1914, he ______ (7.) to New York. He ______ (8.) in a library in New York. In 1918, he ______ (9.) to Argentina.

Pronunciation | simple past *-ed* endings

5a 2.39 Listen and repeat the simple past form of the verbs in the box.

wanted ___	asked ___	moved ___	started ___	finished ___	lived ___	played ___
worked ___	talked ___	closed ___	cooked ___	arrested ___	walked ___	listened ___

b How do you pronounce the *-ed* ending of each verb? Write *t*, *d*, or *id* next to each verb in the box.

c 2.40 Listen and check your answers. Then repeat.

Listening

6 2.41 Listen to "The Story of the Mona Lisa (Part 2)." Mark the sentences true (*T*) or false (*F*).

___ a. The "Mona Lisa" moved to the Louvre.
___ b. It stayed in Napoleon's bedroom.
___ c. The Louvre closed in 1910.
___ d. The police talked to Picasso.
___ e. The police talked to Vincenzo Peruggia.

Grammar | simple past: negatives and questions

7 Complete the Active Grammar box with *did* or *didn't*.

Active Grammar

–	*I/You/He/She/It/We/They*	*didn't stay* *_______ talk*	*in Italy.* *to the police.*	
?	_______	*I/you/he/she/it/we/they*	*stay* *in Italy?* *talk* *to the police?*	*Yes, I/you/he/she/it/we/they _______.* *No, I/you/he/she/it/we/they _______.*

See Reference page 108

8a Use the words to write negative sentences.

1. Picasso/not like/the "Mona Lisa" *Picasso didn't like the* "Mona Lisa."
2. Leonardo da Vinci/not live/Spain _______________
3. the "Mona Lisa"/not stay/Italy _______________

b Use the words to write questions and answers.

1. the police/arrest/Picasso? A: *Did the police arrest Picasso*? B: No, *they didn't*.
2. Andy Warhol/work for/*Vogue*? A: _______________? B: Yes, _______.
3. Van Gogh/move to/London? A: _______________? B: Yes, _______.

Speaking

9 **SPEAKING EXCHANGE** Read the last part of the story on page 110. Ask and answer the questions.

1. Who was the thief?
2. Where was the "Mona Lisa" for two years?
3. How did the thief steal the "Mona Lisa"?

Give a simple summary of a news event

GRAMMAR simple past: irregular verbs

CAN DO

Reading

1a Read the magazine page. Fill in the blanks in each story with *good* or *bad*.

Good Week, Bad Week

1. It was a ____________ week for actor Romero Cline, age 43. He went to Las Vegas last week and he met Monica Hawkins, a waitress in a fast food restaurant. Three days later, they got married.

2. It was a ____________ week for Mr. and Mrs. Blatt from the US. They had fish for dinner, and they found three gold coins inside the fish. "The fish was $3.50," said Mrs. Blatt, "but the gold coins are worth $1,000 each!"

3. It was a ____________ week for pop group Gilt. Gilt's concert was last Friday, but the tickets said "Saturday." "Only five people came and saw the concert," said Sia Kahn, Gilt's singer. "They took photos and bought a T-shirt, but it wasn't a good day."

CROSSWORD*

*(See page 103, Exercise 4)

4. It was a ____________ week for Emiliana Rotman from Sweden. She won €14 million in the Euro lottery, but she lost her ticket. "Never mind," said Emiliana, "That's life!"

b 2.42 Listen and check your answers.

c Mark these statements true (*T*) or false (*F*).

T 1. Romero Cline got married last week.
____ 2. Monica Hawkins works in a restaurant.
____ 3. Emiliana Rotman doesn't have €14 million.
____ 4. Emiliana Rotman is very sad.
____ 5. Gilt's concert was on Saturday.
____ 6. Sia Kahn bought a T-shirt.
____ 7. The Blatts found coins under the fish.
____ 8. Mr. and Mrs. Blatt bought three fish.

2 **Pair Work** Close your books. What can you remember about the four stories?

Grammar | simple past: irregular verbs

3a Look at the magazine page in Exercise 1a on page 102 again. Underline all the verbs in the simple past.

b Complete the Active Grammar box with *take* or *took*.

Active Grammar

+	*I/You/He She/We/They*	***went** to Paris.* *__________ photos.*
−	*I/You/He/ She/We/They*	***didn't go** to Paris.* ***didn't** __________ photos.*
?	***Did*** *I/you/he/ she/we/ they*	***go** to Paris?* *__________ photos?*
	*Yes, I/you/he/she/we/they **did**.* *No, I/you/he/she/we/they **didn't**.*	

See Reference page 108

4 Complete the crossword on page 102 with the simple past form of the regular and irregular verbs below.

ACROSS
3 come 5 play 8 see 9 buy
12 finish 14 have 15 move 16 go

DOWN
1 meet 2 ask 4 listen 6 get
7 win 10 find 11 say 13 lose

5 **Pair Work** Look at the phrases in the box. Which did or didn't you do last week? Tell your partner.

go to a supermarket	lose something
have fish for dinner	find money
come to class late	take a photo
buy new clothes	see a concert

Speaking

6a **Group Work** Ask five people, "How was last week for you?" Ask why.

b **Pair Work** Tell a new partner about the people you talked to.

It was a good week for Pedro. He started a new job, and he went to a concert.

Vocabulary | large numbers

7a Read the How To box. When is *and* used?

How To:

Say large numbers

100	*a hundred/one hundred*
915	*nine hundred and fifteen*
1,000	*a thousand/one thousand*
2,690	*two thousand six hundred and ninety*

b 2.43 Listen and write the prices in the ad.

8 **Pair Work** Now tell your partner the prices.

The DVD player was $199. Now it's $149.

Writing

9 Write a short good week/bad week news story.

Talk about immediate and long-term plans

CAN DO

GRAMMAR *be going to*

Listing

Listening

1 **Pair Work** Ask and answer the questions below.

1. How was your week?
2. What happened in the last seven days?

2a 2.44 Listen and match a person in the photo to their week below. Write the names.

1. an exciting week ____________
2. an interesting week ____________
3. busy week (x2) ____________ ____________

b Listen again. Complete the chart below with notes.

	What happened?	What are his or her plans?
Nick	*talked to manager*	*find a new job*
Abby		
Charlie		
Haley		

Grammar | *be going to*

3 Complete the Active Grammar box with *'s*, *is*, *not*, and *are*. Look at Audioscript 2.44 on page 124 to help you.

Active Grammar

+	*I'm* / *She* ______	*going to*	*get married.* / *find a new job.*
−	*He's* / *They're*	*not going to* / ______ *going to*	*move to Texas.* / *get married soon.*
?	______ *you* / ______ *she*	*going to*	*have a party?* / *see Daniel tonight?*
?	*What* ______ *you* / *Where* ______ *he*	*going to*	*do tomorrow?* / *stay?*

See Reference page 108

4a Look at Nick, Haley, and Charlie's plans for tomorrow. Write complete sentences.

	Nick	Haley and Charlie
tomorrow	~~play football~~ play tennis	~~eat out~~ stay at home
next Sunday	~~write a report~~ stay in bed all day	~~go for a walk~~ have lunch with friends
next Monday	~~work from home~~ visit a customer	~~work~~ take a day off

Nick's not going to play football tomorrow.
He's going to play tennis.

b **Pair Work** Ask questions from the chart above.

c **Pair Work** Tell your partner your plans for next week.

Vocabulary | future plans

5a Match each phrase in the box to a photo.

_____ get in shape	_____ retire	_____ start a business
_____ learn to drive	_____ go to college	_____ have a child/children

1

2

3

4

5

6

b **Pair Work** Which of the phrases did you, your friends, or your family do in the past? Which of these things are you going to do in the future? Tell your partner.

Speaking

6 **Pair Work** Imagine you win $3 million in the lottery. What are you going to do? Make notes and then tell your partner.

Extra Listening Activity in ACTIVEBOOK

Review

1 Complete the email with the simple past form of the verbs in the box.

watch talk cook ~~work~~ visit stay play

Hi Felicia,

How was your weekend? I *worked* (1.) on Saturday ☺ — I have a lot of work at the moment. In the evening, my friend ____________ (2.) dinner for me and we ____________ (3.) a movie. That was nice! On Sunday morning, I ____________ (4.) tennis with my friends, and in the afternoon, my cousin ____________ (5.) me. He lives in Taipei. We ____________ (6.) at home and ____________ (7.) about our lives. He's very happy in Taipei.

Hope you're OK. Send me an email soon!

Kayo

2 Use the words to write complete sentences in the simple past.

1. My friend/start/a new job
   My friend started a new job.
2. Julio/move/to America?
   ____________?
3. I/not talk/to my boss
   ____________.
4. you/play chess/with Michelle?
   ____________?
5. Mei and I/cook/dinner
   ____________.
6. Paul/not like/his present
   ____________.

3 **Pair Work** Work with a partner. Find the simple past form of the verbs below in the word grid.

1. have
2. find
3. take
4. meet
5. give
6. steal
7. go
8. say

e	y	u	b	f	l
m	e	t	o	o	k
s	a	i	d	u	k
t	a	z	g	n	m
o	g	h	a	d	v
l	j	f	v	d	f
e	s	w	e	n	t

4 Complete each sentence with the simple past form of the verb in parentheses.

1. How *did* you *break* your arm? (break)
2. They ____________ a lot of money. (win)
3. Why ____________ the police ____________ them? (arrest)
4. Your mother ____________ to the supermarket. (go)

5 Write questions to find the missing information. Then practice with a partner. Make up answers.

1. __?__'s going to retire.
   Who's going to retire?
2. I'm going to buy a __?__.
   What are you going to buy?
3. They're going to __?__.
   ____________?
4. I'm going to call __?__.
   ____________?
5. Lucy's going to go to __?__ University.
   ____________?
6. Tom and Minnie are going to move to __?__.
   ____________?

Communication | talk about past and future vacations

6a Think about your favorite vacation from your past. Answer the questions.

1. When was it? ________________
2. Where did you go? ________________
3. Who did you go with? ________________
4. How long did you stay? ________________
5. Where did you stay (hotel, B&B, etc.)? ________________
6. What did you do? ________________

b **Pair Work** Use your notes to tell your partner about your vacation.

My favorite vacation was in 2010. I went to South Africa with my wife, and we went on a safari. We stayed for two weeks and . . .

7a **Pair Work** What places are in the photos? Which places would you like to visit? What other places would you really like to visit?

b Imagine you and your partner win a vacation of a lifetime. Read the rules.

The Rules

1. It is a two-week vacation.
2. You can fly to three different places.
3. You always travel together.

c **Pair Work** Plan your vacation. Choose three destinations and make notes on:

1. where (**Ex:** Beijing, China)
2. how long (**Ex:** four days)
3. plans (**Ex:** eat Chinese food, see the palace)

How about Beijing?

Yes, good idea. I want to go there. How long are we going to stay?

8 **Pair Work** Find a new partner. Explain your vacation plans to your new partner.

First, we're going to fly to Beijing, China. We're going to stay there for four days. We're going to see the Forbidden City and we're going to eat Chinese food. Then we're going to fly to . . .

Unit 10 Reference

Simple past

Regular verbs

+		
I		
You		
He	lived	in Rome.
She	worked	with my sister.
It	stayed	in a nice hotel.
We		
They		

To make the simple past of regular verbs, add *-ed* or *-d* to the end of the verb.

Irregular verbs

+		
I		
You		
He	saw	a new camera.
She	bought	a nice car.
It	had	a computer.
We		
They		

A lot of verbs are irregular in the simple past affirmative; for example:

buy—bought	*come—came*	*do—did*
eat—ate	*find—found*	*get—got*
give—gave	*go—went*	*have—had*
make—made	*read /rid/—read /rɛd/*	
say—said	*see—saw*	*speak—spoke*
win—won	*write—wrote*	

−		
I		
You		
He	didn't talk	to Cynthia.
She	didn't listen	to the pop star.
It	didn't go	out.
We		
They		

Use *didn't* + verb to make the negative. Do not use the past form in the negative.

~~She didn't went to the concert.~~

She didn't go to the concert.

?			
	I		
	you	move	
	he	walk	to work?
Did	she		to school?
	it	go	to London?
	we	come	
	they		

Use *Did* + subject + verb to make questions. Do not use the past form in the question.

~~Did they moved to Paris?~~

Did they move to Paris?

be going to

Use *going to* + verb to talk about plans for the future.

−	I	'm		
	You	're		
	He She It	's	going to not going to	get in shape. retire. get married.
	We	're		
	They	're		
?	Am	I		
	Are	you		
	Is	he she it	going to	take the bus? visit my sister?
	Are	we		
	Are	they		

Unit Vocabulary

Verbs + nouns

steal a cell phone	lose your wallet
break your arm	win the lottery
move to a new house	find money
meet a famous person	stay in bed

Future plans

get in shape	learn to drive
go to college	have a child/children
start a new business	retire

Speaking Exchange

Unit 8 | Page 85, Exercise 8

Students B and C

Salt and Pepper
Menu

APPETIZERS
Chicken salad
Vegetable soup
House salad
Seafood cocktail

MAIN COURSES
Beef with vegetables and rice
Lamb chops with rice
Roast chicken with potatoes
Seafood pasta
Fish with vegetables and rice

DESSERTS
Chocolate ice cream
Chocolate cake
Cheese and fruit

Unit 6 | Page 63, Exercise 7

Student A

Name: Sandra Young

From: the US

Live in: Vancouver, Canada

Reason here: business

Job: Sales rep (sell suitcases and backpacks to stores)

Work for: The Big Bag Company

Work where: near Vancouver

Husband: William Young (Student B)

Student B

Name: William Young

From: Australia

Live in: Vancouver, Canada

Reason here: business

Job: Sales rep (sell tea and coffee to supermarkets)

Work for: Love Coffee Company

Work where: in Vancouver

Wife: Sandra Young (Student A)

Unit 7 | Page 71, Exercise 8b

See page 111 for answers.

Unit 10 | Page 101, Exercise 9

The Story of the Mona Lisa (PART 3)

Two years later, the police arrested Vincenzo Peruggia. He was the thief. But how did he steal the "Mona Lisa"?

Vincenzo was in the Louvre on August 21, 1911. The museum was very quiet. When Vincenzo walked out, the "Mona Lisa" was under his coat. The painting stayed in Vincenzo's apartment, near the Louvre, for two years. In 1913, Vincenzo wanted to sell the painting. He wanted to sell it in Italy. The police arrested him in Milan.

Unit 8 | Page 87, Exercise 6

Student A

Person	Address
Mr. M. Haddon	7 Oak Lane, 10a
Ms. A. Walker	7 Oak Lane, 9b
Ms. Z. Smith	7 Oak Lane, 8c
Mr. J. Heller	7 Oak Lane, 7b
Mr. S. Kato	7 Oak Lane, 7a

Unit 8 | Page 82, Exercise 3c

A good present for Pablo's sister: money

Unit 8 | Page 87, Exercise 6

Student B

Ms. M. Atwood	7 Oak Lane, 7c
Mr. J. Coe	7 Oak Lane, 8b
Ms. T. Morrison	7 Oak Lane, 8a
Mr. O. Pamuk	7 Oak Lane, 9c
Mrs. A. Garcia	7 Oak Lane, 9a

Unit 6 | Page 61, Exercise 6b

Student B

1. big cities
2. hip hop music
3. Nicole Kidman and Keith Urban
4. museums
5. Julia Roberts
6. Bill Gates
7. the countryside

Unit 7 | Page 71, Exercise 8b

Answers:

1. October/Fall
2. January/Winter
3. April/Spring
4. July/Summer

Unit 6 | Page 63, Exercise 7

Student C

Name:	Keiko Price
From:	Japan
Live in:	Tokyo, Japan
Reason here:	vacation
Job:	Bag designer
Work for:	Bags R Us
Work where:	in Tokyo
Husband:	Ron Price (Student D)

Student D

Name:	Ron Price
From:	the UK
Live in:	Tokyo, Japan
Reason here:	vacation
Job:	English teacher
Work for:	Gotham English school
Work where:	in Tokyo
Wife:	Keiko Price (Student C)

Unit 6 | Page 67, Exercise 8

findanicepresent.com

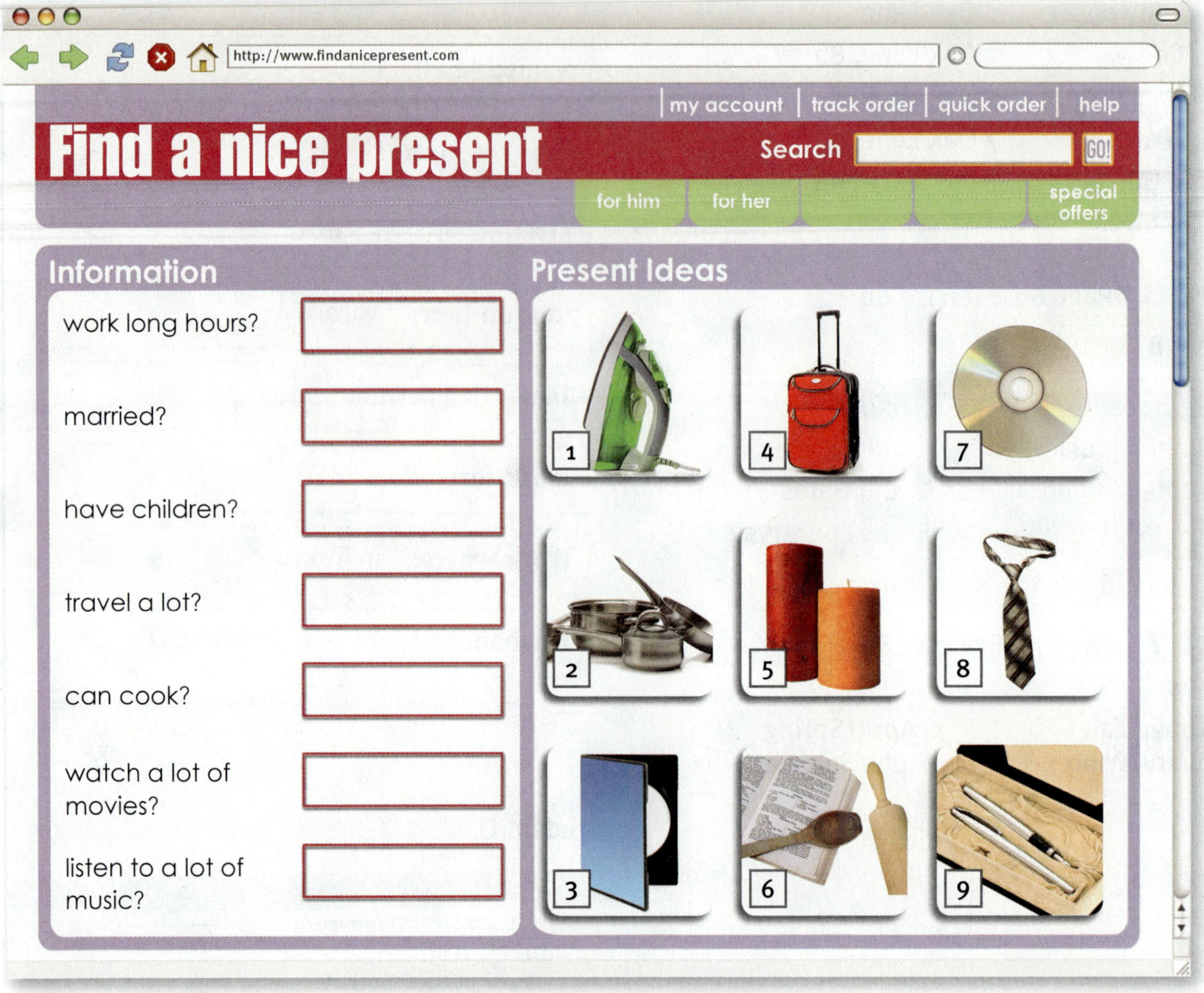

Unit 8 | Page 83, Exercise 6

Read the quiz questions. Check (✓) A, B, or C.

A = Yes, I do.

B = No, but I want one.

C = No, and I don't want one.

Technology Quiz	A	B	C
1. Do you have a computer?			
2. Do you have an MP3 player?			
3. Do you have a digital camera?			
4. Do you have a camera-phone?			
5. Do you have a phone with apps?			
6. Do you have a flat-screen TV?			
7. Do you have broadband on your TV?			
8. Do you have a GPS device?			
9. Do you have an e-book reader?			

Start
The "my first my last" Game
1. my first bicycle
2. my last visit to the movies
3. my first best friend
4. my last night in a hotel
5. my first day at school
6. my last CD
7. my first CD
8. my last visit to a museum
9. my first computer
10. my first camera
11. my last book
12. my first cell phone
13. my last visit to a tourist attraction
14. my first vacation
Finish

Writing Bank

A vacation email

Write a subject for your email.

Begin the email: *Hi* or *Hello* + name,

Talk about the place: your hotel/the town, etc. Use contractions: *we're, it's, . . .*

Explain any attachments.

From: louisebrown@umail.com
To: claudia2000@wowmail.com
Subject: We're on vacation!
Attachment: JPG (0.22 MB) JPG (0.16 MB)

Hi Claudia,

How are you?

We're on vacation in Switzerland. We're in Lausanne. Our hotel is The Atlantis Hotel. It's great. Lausanne is small and beautiful. It's on Lake Geneva.

The two attachments are photos. Photo 1 is Jason and me. We're at Lake Geneva. Photo 2 is Jason in our hotel room.

See you on Tuesday!

Love,
Louise

The first sentence: *How are you?* or *Thanks for your email.*

End the email: *See you on* + day or *See you soon* or *Hope to see you soon.*

For your close to friends, write *Love,* + your name. For other people, write *Best wishes,* + your name.

Writing tip | punctuation

. = period ? = a question mark

, = a comma ' = an apostrophe

A, B, C, etc. = capital letters

Periods

Use a period at the end of a sentence.

- *Our hotel is The Atlantis Hotel.*

Capital letters

Use a capital letter at the beginning of a sentence.

- *The two attachments are photos.*

Use capital letters for the names of people, places, days, months, books, and movies.

- *My favorite author is Hemingway.*
- *See you on Thursday.*

Use a capital letter for the pronoun *I*.

- *Can I have a cup of coffee, please?*

Use capital letters for countries, nationalities, and languages.

- *She's from Spain. She's Spanish.*

Commas

Use commas in lists.

- *It's small, old, and beautiful.*
- *The attachment is a photo of Laura, Adam, and Sarah.*

Use a comma before *please* and after *yes* and *no*.

- *What's your name, please?*
- A: *Coffee?* B: *No, thank you.*

Apostrophes

Use an apostrophe to show a contraction.

- *We are on vacation.* → *We're on vacation.*

Use an apostrophe + *s* to show possession.

- *Do you like Jason's car?*
- *They are Susan's books.*

A description | my favorite place to visit

My favorite place to visit is New York City. ← Use capital letters for cities and countries: *New York, Mexico City, Japan*, etc.
It's on the East Coast. There are a lot of museums, shops, restaurants, and other tourist attractions.

Use apostrophe + *s* (*'s*) to show possession: *New York's parks, Seoul's museums*, etc. → New York's parks are great. Central Park is in the center of New York. It's very big, and in summer there are concerts in the park. Bryant Park is beautiful, too. It's a small park near Grand Central Station.

The Metropolitan Museum is very popular. ← Use adjectives to describe a place: *popular, great, modern, beautiful, old*, etc.
It's very big, and the building is beautiful. But I think The Museum of Modern Art is New York's top attraction. It's in Midtown, near Fifth Avenue. The exhibitions are great!

The Empire State Building is a popular tourist attraction. It's a very tall building.
Talk about location: *in, on, near, next to*, etc. → It's in Midtown, near Times Square. It's expensive, but the views of New York are amazing.

Writing tip | *and, but*

Use *and* before the last item in a list.

- *There are a lot of museums, shops, restaurants, and other tourist attractions.*
- *It's very big, very old, and very popular.*
- *He's an actor and a teacher.*

Use *and* to join two similar sentences.

- *The country is beautiful. The beaches are great.*
  → *The country is beautiful, and the beaches are great.*
- *Central Park is very big. There are concerts in the park.*
  → *Central Park is very big, and there are concerts in the park.*

Use *but* to join two different (contrasting) sentences.

- *The country is beautiful. The beaches are awful.*
  → *The country is beautiful, but the beaches are awful.*
- *There's a museum in the town. There isn't a theme park.*
  → *There's a museum in the town, but there isn't a theme park.*

A letter to a friend

15 Westbrook Road
Boston, MA 02118

Write your address here.

Write the date here.

September 24, 2011

Begin the letter: *Dear* + name,

Dear Fatima,

How are you? Long time, no see!

First paragraph: *How are you?* or *I hope all is well.*

I live in Boston now. My new address is at the top of this letter. I'm a designer at a computer company, and Jeremy is a manager at a department store. Life is good, and I'm very happy. I get up at 7 o'clock and eat breakfast, but Jeremy gets up at 9 o'clock. He starts work at 10 o'clock. We finish work at 6 o'clock, and Jeremy cooks dinner. In the evening, we watch TV or read a book.

Join two sentences with *and* or *but*.

Ask about his or her life.

How is your life? Are you still a builder?

End the letter.

Please write and tell me your news.

Love,
Fran

For close friends, write *Love,* or *From,* + your name.

For other people, write *Best wishes,* + your name.

Writing tip | spelling of verbs in the simple present with *he/she/it*

With *he, she,* and *it,* add *-s* to the verb.

- *I get up early. He gets up late.*
- *I start work at nine o'clock. She starts work at ten o'clock.*

For verbs ending in *-ch, -sh, -s, -x, -z,* and *-o,* add *-es* to the verb with *he, she,* and *it.*

- *They watch TV. She watches TV.*
- *I finish work at five o'clock. She finishes work at six o'clock.*

For verbs ending in consonant + *-y,* change *y* to *i* and add *-es.*

- *I carry the big bags, and my brother carries the small bags.*

For verbs ending in vowel + *-y,* add *s.*

- *I play tennis, and my sister plays basketball.*

A formal email

Write a subject for your email.

From: amywatson@mymail.com
To: waterbridgehotel@wowmail.com
Subject: Room for June 3rd/4th

Begin the email: *Dear* + name,

Dear Waterbridge Hotel,

Don't use contractions.

I would like some more information about your hotel.

- Is there a room available on Saturday June 3 and Sunday June 4?
- How much is the room for two nights?
- Is breakfast included?
- Is there a swimming pool at the hotel?

End the email with *I look forward to your reply.*

I look forward to your reply.

For formal letters and emails, end with *Sincerely*, or *Best wishes*, + your name.

Sincerely,
Amy Watson

Writing tip | formal English and informal English

These are the main differences between formal English and informal English in writing.

INFORMAL **Writing to a friend**	**FORMAL** **Writing to a business contact**
Start with: • *Hi* + first name, **NOTE:** we don't use • ~~*Dear Friend,*~~ • ~~*Hi Friend,*~~	Start with: • *Dear* + *Mr./Mrs./Miss/Ms.* + last name, When you don't know the person's name, start with: • *Dear Sir or Madam,*
Before you end the email use: • *See you soon.* • *Speak to you soon.*	Before you end the email, use: • *I look forward to your reply.* • *I look forward to hearing from you soon.*
End with: • *Love,* • *Take care,* When you don't know the person very well, end with: • *Best,* • *Best wishes,*	End with: • *Sincerely,* • *Best wishes,*
Use contractions: • *I'm, you're, they're,* etc.	Do not use contractions. Use: • *I am, you are, they are,* etc. **NOTE:** It is OK to use *don't*.

Pronunciation Bank

Part 1 | 2.45 English phonemes

Consonants

Symbol	Key word	Symbol	Key word
d	date	ŋ	going
b	bed	s	sofa
t	ten	z	zero
p	park	ʃ	shop
k	car	ʒ	television
g	game	h	hat
tʃ	child	m	menu
dʒ	job	n	near
f	four	l	like
v	visit	r	ride
θ	three	y	young
ð	this	w	wife

Vowels

Symbol	Key word	Symbol	Key word
i	be	ə	about
ɪ	sit	eɪ	day
ɛ	red	aɪ	by
æ	cat	aʊ	house
ɑ	father	ɔɪ	boy
oʊ	boat	ɑr	car
ɔ	bought	ɔr	door
ʊ	book	ʊr	tour
u	shoe	ɪr	here
ʌ	but	ɛr	there
ɚ	word		

Part 2 | 2.46 Sound-spelling correspondences

Sound	Spelling	Examples
/ɪ/	i	this listen
	y	gym typical
	ui	build guitar
	e	pretty
/i/	ee	green sleep
	ie	niece believe
	ea	read teacher
	e	these complete
	ey	key money
	ei	receipt receive
	i	police
/æ/	a	can man land
/ɑ/	a	pasta
	al	calm
	ea	heart
/ʌ/	u	fun sunny husband
	o	some mother month
	ou	cousin double young
/ɔ/	ou	bought
	au	daughter taught
	al	bald small always
	aw	draw jigsaw
/aɪ/	i	like time island
	y	dry shy cycle
	ie	fries die tie
	igh	light high right
	ei	height
	ey	eyes
	uy	buy
/ɛɪ/	a	lake hate shave
	ai	wait train straight
	ay	play say stay
	ey	they obey
	ei	eight weight
	ea	break
/oʊ/	o	home phone open
	ow	show throw own
	oa	coat road coast
	ol	cold told

Part 3 | ▶ 2.47 Syllable stress

Words with more than one syllable have the stress on one of the syllables.

1-syllable words ●	2-syllable words ●○	2-syllable words ○●
one six big young read learn friend great lake house beach road west	happy seven listen morning passport father website photo awful teacher picture modern Sunday	Japan address between today behind Chinese design July explain mistake dessert because
3-syllable words ●○○	**3-syllable words ○●○**	**3-syllable words ○○●**
Italy favorite beautiful Saturday visitor medium popular interview architect hospital	eleven computer cathedral espresso attachment important piano designer reporter together September tomorrow exciting potato	afternoon engineer introduce

Part 4 | ▶ 2.48 Questions

We often use weak forms at the beginning of questions.

Are you at home?	/ər yə/
Are they ready?	/ər ðeɪ/
Do you like it?	/də yə/
Do you write reports?	/də yə/
What do you do?	wədiya
Where do they work?	wɛrdiyə
Are you going to get married?	/ər yə goʊɪŋ tə/
	or /ər yə gənə/
Are you going to call her?	/ər yə goʊɪŋ tə/
	or /ər yə gənə/
Were you a good student?	/wɚr yə/
Did you see him?	/dɪ dʒə/
Did you talk to her?	/dɪ dʒə/

Irregular Verbs

Verb	Simple Past	Past Participle	Verb	Simple Past	Past Participle
be	was/were	been	leave	left	left
become	became	become	let	let	let
begin	began	begun	lose	lost	lost
break	broke	broken	make	made	made
bring	brought	brought	mean	meant	meant
build	built	built	meet	met	met
buy	bought	bought	pay	paid	paid
can	could	been able	put	put	put
catch	caught	caught	read/rid/	read/red/	read/red/
choose	chose	chosen	ride	rode	ridden
come	came	come	ring	rang	rung
cost	cost	cost	run	ran	run
dig	dug	dug	say	said	said
do	did	done	see	saw	seen
draw	drew	drawn	sell	sold	sold
drink	drank	drunk	send	sent	sent
drive	drove	driven	shine	shone	shone
eat	ate	eaten	show	showed	shown
fall	fell	fallen	sing	sang	sung
feed	fed	fed	sit	sat	sat
feel	felt	felt	sleep	slept	slept
find	found	found	speak	spoke	spoken
fly	flew	flown	spend	spent	spent
forget	forgot	forgotten	stand	stood	stood
get	got	got	steal	stole	stolen
give	gave	given	swim	swam	swum
go	went	gone/been	take	took	taken
grow	grew	grown	teach	taught	taught
have	had	had	tell	told	told
hear	heard	heard	think	thought	thought
hold	held	held	throw	threw	thrown
hurt	hurt	hurt	understand	understood	understood
keep	kept	kept	wear	wore	worn
know	knew	known	win	won	won
learn	learned/learnt	learned/learnt	write	wrote	written

Audioscript

UNIT 6 All about you

2.03 (Page 60)

DJ= Disk Jockey JDS= João da Silva

DJ: Now it's time for our 60-second interview.
Today João da Silva is in the studio. Welcome to *Radio Chicago*, João.
JDS: Thank you.
DJ: João . . . your 60-second interview starts . . . now.
DJ: So, João What do you do? What's your occupation?
JDS: I'm a singer.
DJ: Where are you from?
JDS: I'm from Bahia, but Rio de Janeiro is my home now.
DJ: Do you like Chicago?
JDS: Yes, I do. It's very nice.
DJ: You're a singer. Do you like American hip hop music?
JDS: No, not really. I like Brazilian music, especially samba.
DJ: OK. What's your favorite sport?
JDS: Soccer, of course! I'm Brazilian.
DJ: Of course. What about food? Do you like Indian food?
JDS: No, I don't. I like French food.
DJ: What are your favorite things in life?
JDS: I like Brazilian music, German cars, Italian fashion . . .
DJ: Ah! Time is up. Thank you João da Silva!
JDS: You're welcome.
DJ: That was our 60-second interview!

2.04 (Page 60)

1. Do you like Italian food?
2. Do you like coffee?
3. Are you from Brazil?
4. Are you a student?

2.06 (Page 62)

1. Architects design buildings.
2. Sales reps sell things.
3. Fashion designers design clothes.
4. Reporters write articles.
5. Chefs cook food.
6. Construction workers build buildings.

2.07 (Page 62)

S=Sharon C=Catherine
P=Pat A=Anthony

S: Excuse me. Your coat is on the floor.
C: Pardon?
S: Your coat. It's on the floor.
C: Oh, yeah. Thanks a lot.
S: No problem! Are you here on vacation?
C: Yes, I am. I'm here with my husband. He's in our room. We really like this city.
S: Yes, it's great. By the way, my name's Sharon.
C: Hi, Sharon. I'm Catherine.
S: So where are you from?
C: I'm from Canada and my husband is from Australia. We live in Toronto. Where are you from?
S: We're from the US. We live in Seattle.
C: Are you here on vacation?
S: No, we aren't. We're here on business.
C: What do you do?
S: We're architects.
C: That's nice. What kinds of things do you design?
S: We design houses and office buildings.
C: I'm a sales rep and my husband is a chef.
S: Oh, really? What do you sell?
C: I sell clothing to department stores.
P: And who do you work for?
C: It's a small Canadian company. It's called PDS Fashions.
S: Oh, I'm sorry. This is my husband, Pat.
C: Nice to meet you. My name's Catherine. Ah! Here's my husband. Anthony, this is Sharon and Pat. They're from the US.
A: Nice to meet you.
P: Nice to meet you, too.
C: Sharon and Pat are architects. They design houses and office buildings.
A: Oh really? Where do you work?

2.08 (Page 67)

J=Jim N=Nancy

J: Oh, man!
N: What's the problem, Jim?
J: I can't find a present for Luz.
N: Who's Luz?
J: She's my friend. It's her birthday on Thursday.
N: Do you know www.findanicepresent.com?
J: No. What is it?
N: It's a great website. It finds presents for you. Look. This is the website.

2.09 (Page 67)

J=Jim N=Nancy

J: Is it free?
N: Yes, it is. OK, there are some questions here. Tell me about Luz. How old is she?
J: She's, um, twenty-nine.
N: And what does she do?
J: She's a reporter.
N: Who does she work for?
J: *Newstime* magazine.
N: She's a reporter. OK. So does she work long hours?
J: Yes, she does.
N: Is she married?
J: No, she isn't.
N: What about children? Does she have any children?
J: No, she doesn't.
N: How about travel? Does she travel a lot?
J: Yes. She travels all over the world.
N: She's lucky. Can she cook?
J: No, she can't.
N: How about movies? Does she watch a lot of movies?
J: Let me think. No, she doesn't.
N: Does she listen to a lot of music?
J: Yes. She loves music.
N: OK—there are three good presents on this website.

UNIT 7 A day at work

2.10 (Page 69)

1. F. I'm a waiter. I work in a restaurant.
2. A. I'm an office worker. I work in an office.
3. G. I'm a factory worker. I work in a factory.
4. B. I'm a nurse. I work in a hospital.
5. E. I'm a sales clerk. I work in a shop.
6. C. I'm a professor. I work in a university.
7. D. I'm a researcher. I work in a lab.
8. H. I'm a teacher. I work in a school.

2.11 (Page 70)

1.

R=Receptionist J=Jake A=Alice S=Steven

R: Hello. Parkside School.
J: Can I speak to Mrs. Fisher, please?
R: Hold on, please.
A: Hello. Alice Fisher.
J: Hello, Mrs. Fisher. My name's Jake Parker. I'm interested in the teaching job. It's in today's newspaper . . .
A: Oh, yes. Great.

2.

A: Jake Parker?
J: Yes.
A: I'm Alice Fisher. Nice to meet you.
J: Nice to meet you, too.
A: Come in, Mr. Parker. Please sit down.
J: Thank you.

3.

J: OK, class, be quiet. Look at page 32 in your books. Page 32. OK? Now listen to the conversation.
J: Steven. Please turn off your cell phone.
S: Sorry.

2.12 (Page 71)

M=Man W=Woman

1.

M: Please come with me. Your table is ready.

2.

W: Taylor! Be QUIET.

3.

W: This is a message for Dr. Morgan. Please go to Room 200 immediately.

4.

M: This is a customer announcement. Visit our great kitchen sale on the ground floor. Saucepans for nineteen ninety-nine, cookbooks for six ninety-nine. Thank you for shopping at Madisons.

5.

W: This is a message for all passengers on flight FH453 to Hong Kong. Please go to gate 23 immediately. That's flight FH453. Please go to gate 23 immediately. Thank you.

2.14 (Page 72)

H=Game show host J=John

H: I'm Susan Sullivan and welcome to *What's your job?* Today we have John with us. Hi, John. Are you ready?
J: Yes, I'm always ready!

H: OK, let's start. Do you attend meetings?
J: Yes, I sometimes attend meetings.
H: Do you give presentations?
J: Yes, I often give presentations.
H: Do you call customers?
J: Yes, I usually call customers.
H: Do you write reports?
J: Yes, I do, but I don't often write reports.
H: Do you travel for work?
J: Yes, I sometimes travel for work.
H: Do you answer the phone?
J: Yes, I always answer the phone.
H: Do you work outside?
J: No, I never work outside.
H: Do you help people?
J: Yes, I often help people.
H: Are you a . . . sales rep?
J: Yes, I am!

2.16 (Page 74)
M=Michelle S=Sarah
M: Good morning, Sarah!
S: Morning, Michelle. Nice weekend?
M: Yes, thank you. And you?
S: Good, thanks.
M: Oh, Sarah, when is Mr. Wu's visit?
S: Let me see. Mr. Wu's visit is June 8th.
M: What's the date today?
S: It's June 6th.
M: Are there any other visits this month?
S: Um, yes, there are. There's Mrs. King on June 14th.
M: Mrs. King – June 14th.
S: And there's Ms. Brown on June 24th.
M: OK, June 24th. Is that all?
S: No, there's one more. It's Mr. Rodriguez.
M: Mr. Rodriguez – he's the big boss from Bogotá! He's very important! When is his visit?
S: June 6th.
M: June 6th?! . . . But, but that's today.
S: Uh-huh. Hello, Sarah Walker speaking. Hello Mr. Rodriguez. You're at the reception desk? Great. See you in five minutes. Goodbye. That's Mr. Rodriguez. He's at the reception desk.
M: Ugh!

2.18 (Page 75)
M=Michelle R=Mr. Rodriguez K=Ms. Khan
M: Please, come in. Have a seat. What would you like to drink? Tea? Coffee?
R: I'd like coffee.
K: I'd like a cup of tea, please.
M: Would you like milk or sugar?
R: No, thank you.
K: Milk, no sugar, please.

2.19 (Page 75)
M=Michelle R=Mr. Rodriguez K=Ms. Khan
M: All right. Well, this is the company cafeteria. Are you hungry?
R/K: Yes.
M: Good. OK, the drinks are here on the right. And there are snacks next to the drinks. There's bottled water, orange juice, etc. There are some appetizers next to the snacks. Would you like an appetizer?
R: Um, no thank you. I think I'd like a salad.
M: OK. There's a salad bar in the middle of the cafeteria.
K: I'd like some fruit.
M: The fruit is over there, next to the salad. And there are some desserts next to the cash register.
R: Great. Thank you.

2.20 (Page 77)
R=Receptionist WJL= Woo-jin Lee
R: Good morning. Can I help you?
WJL: Good morning. I'm here to see Martina Hafner.
R: Do you have an appointment?
WJL: Yes.
R: What's your name, please?
WJL: Woo-jin Lee.
R: How do you spell that?
WJL: W-O-O J-I-N Lee. L-E-E.
R: OK, Mr. Lee. Take the elevator to the third floor. Turn right. Ms. Hafner's office is the third door on the left.
WJL: Thank you.
R: You're welcome.

R=Receptionist J=James
R: Good morning.
J: Good morning. I have a meeting with Lorda Romero.
R: What's your name, please?
J: James Wood.
R: James – Wood. OK, Mr. Wood. Take the elevator to the third floor. Turn right. Mrs. Romero's office is the second on the right.
J: Thank you.

R=Receptionist J=Jessica
R: Good afternoon.
J: Good afternoon. I'm here to see Patrick Swinton.
R: Do you have an appointment?
J: Yes, I do.
R: What's your name, please?
J: My name's Jessica Hayes.
R: How do you spell Hayes?
J: H – A – Y – E – S.
R: OK, Ms. Hayes. Mr. Swinton's office is on the third floor. Take the elevator and turn right. It's the first door on the left.
J: Thank you.

UNIT 8 Your likes and dislikes

2.21 (Page 79)
1. go to the theater 2. go out to eat
3. play chess 4. go swimming
5. play soccer 6. go hiking
7. watch TV 8. go sightseeing
9. read a book 10. play tennis
11. go cycling 12. work out

2.22 (Page 80)
G=Gary A=Annie
A: Gary.
G: Yeah?
A: Are you happy?
G: Happy?
A: Yes. Are you happy?
G: Yeah. I'm happy.
A: I'm not. I'm bored. We never go out.
G: Oh.
A: We never go to the theater. We don't go sightseeing or stay at hotels. We never go out to eat. We always just stay home and watch television.
G: But I like watching television.
A: Gary!

2.23 (Page 80)
G=Gary A=Annie
G: OK . . . So, let's go away next weekend.
A: Go away?
G: Yes. What about going to Yosemite? We can go hiking, we can see the views. We can go biking, or go swimming.
A: Hmm . . . I don't want to go hiking. I want to go out to eat, I want to go shopping, I want to go to the theater. What about San Francisco?
G: San Francisco?
A: Yes, we can go sightseeing and see the city. You like to go sightseeing.
G: Yes, but, I don't like to go sightseeing in cities. I like going hiking, swimming, playing tennis—outdoor things.
A: Hmm . . . Well what about Palm Springs? You can go swimming—you like to swim. And we can play tennis, maybe some golf. And I can go shopping. And we can go out to eat.
G: You like to go out to eat . . . OK, I want to go to Palm Springs.

2.24 (Page 80)
I want to go out to eat.
I want to go shopping.
I want to go to the theater.
I don't want to go hiking.

2.25 (Page 82)
J. dishwasher N. coffee table
G. mirror L. sofa M. lamp
E. toilet B. bed P. car F. sink
Q. bicycle I. cabinet K. fridge
D. bathtub A. window H. stove
C. wardrobe O. armchair

2.26 (Page 82)
P=Pablo J=Jo
P: Hi, Jo. How are you?
J: Oh, hi Pablo. I'm fine. How are you?
P: Oh, so-so. It's my sister's wedding next week and I want to buy her a really nice present, but I can't find one.
J: I can help.
P: Really?
J: Sure.
P: Thanks a lot.
J: No problem. What does she like doing?
P: Well, she likes doing things at home: she likes watching TV, she likes cooking. Oh, and she likes modern furniture. Her husband likes furniture, too.
J: Do they have an armchair?
P: Yes, they do.
J: Do they have a lamp?
P: Yes, they do.
J: Does your sister have a nice sofa?
P: No, she doesn't.
J: Buy her a sofa.

P: But my parents want to buy a nice sofa for her.
J: Oh, too bad. Well, do they have a coffee table?
P: Yes.
J: Okay, then does she have a bicycle?
P: No, she doesn't.
J: There you are.
P: But he has a bicycle and she uses it.
J: Oh . . . I know!
P: What?
J: It's always a good wedding present.
P: What?
J: Give them . . .

2.27 (Page 84)
M=Mark A=Anna
M: Hi, Anna.
A: Hi, Mark. What's new?
M: I got a new job!
A: Hey, that's great! Congratulations. How about dinner next Friday? We can celebrate.
M: Good idea. Which restaurant do you want to go to?
A: How about Sinatra's?
M: Where's that?
A: It's in Melrose.
M: Hmm, that's pretty far. What about Wasabi?
A: Wasabi? What kind of food do they serve?
M: Japanese food.
A: Hmm. How big is it?
M: It's pretty big.
A: Oh, I don't really like big restaurants. I know! What about Carlito's? My friend is the manager there.
M: Who is your friend?
A: Thomas. You know, Thomas.
M: Oh yeah. OK. Carlito's is good.

2.28 (Page 85)
1. chicken 2. seafood 3. fish
4. potatoes 5. lamb 6. rice 7. cheese
8. beef 9. pasta 10. chocolate

2.29 (Page 85)
W=Waiter A=Anna M=Mark
W: Hello. Do you have a reservation?
A: Yes. My name is Anna Pierce.
W: Ms. Pierce. A table for two?
A: That's right.
W: Come with me, please.
(later)
W: Are you ready to order?
M: Yes. I'd like the fish soup, please, and the lamb chops.
W: Certainly, sir. And for you ma'am?
A: I'd like the seafood cocktail, please, and the vegetable pasta.
W: Certainly. What would you like to drink?
M: Bottled water, please.
A: And can I get orange juice, please?
W: Certainly.
(later)
M: Oh, look at the time. It's pretty late.
A: Oh, my. It's 10:30.
M: Yes, it is. Excuse me. Can I have the check, please?
W: Of course.

UNIT 9 Your life

2.30 (Page 89)
First iPod in Stores: 2002
William and Kate – Royal Wedding: 2011
Tsunami in Southeast Asia: 2004
Titanic Disaster: 1912
Haiti Earthquake: 2010
Martin Luther King – I have a dream: 1963
Juan Peron: President of Argentina: 1946
Elvis Presley is dead: 1977

2.31 (Page 91)
I was an actor.
You were a singer.
He was happy.
She was born in 1982.
It was great.
We were singers.
They were rich.

2.32 (Page 92)
ML= Mei Ling I= Isabella K= Kenji
ML: OK. Your turn, Kenji.
K: Four! One, two, three, four. My first teacher!
I: OK, Kenji. Your first teacher. Forty-five seconds. Starting now!
K: OK, my first teacher was Mrs. Lloyd. She was about fifty years old.
ML: Was she a good teacher?
K: She was a good teacher, but I wasn't a good student.
I: Were you her favorite student?
K: I wasn't her favorite student. Koji was her favorite student.
ML: Was Koji your friend?
K: Yes, he . . . Oh no!
ML: Too bad, Kenji. OK, Isabella, your turn.
I: Two! One, two. Your last meal at a restaurant.
ML: OK, Isabella. Your last meal at a restaurant. Forty-five seconds. Starting now!
I: OK, my last meal at a restaurant was last week at Carluccio's.
K: Oh – that's great.
I: Yes, and . . . Oh no!
ML: Too bad, Isabella. OK, my turn. Five! One, two, three, four, five. My last vacation.
K: OK, Mei Ling Your last vacation. Forty-five seconds. Starting NOW!
ML: My last vacation was two years ago. It was to a Pacific island called Palau.
K: Were you with your parents?
ML: I wasn't with my parents. I was with my friend, Helen.
I: Was it a good vacation?
ML: It was a very good vacation. The hotel was very nice.
I: Were there any tourist attractions? Castles or palaces or . . .?
ML: There weren't any castles or palaces, but there were some beautiful beaches.
I: Was the weather nice?
ML: It was great. Sunny and hot . . .
K: Time's up! That's forty-five seconds. Good job, Mei Ling.
I: Yes, good job. Your turn again.
ML: Oh great! Six! One, two . . .

2.34 (Page 94)
4. do the laundry 2. clean the bathroom
1. vacuum the house 3. wash the dishes
6. cook dinner 5. iron a shirt

2.35 (Page 95)
AD=Aunt Dorothy J=Jeff B=Billy K=Karen F=Friend
1.
AD: Hello, Jeff. How are you?
J: Fine, thank you, Aunt Dorothy. How was your flight?
AD: Awful. Awful. There wasn't any coffee. There was no movie. And the flight was late. I'm so tired. Could you carry my suitcases? There are three.
J: Uh, yeah, sure.
2.
J: So, how was school, Billy?
B: Good!
J: Were you good for your teacher?
B: No! I was very bad! It was funny. Daddy, can I have ice cream for dinner?
J: No. Ice cream's not good for dinner.
3.
K: Hi, Jeff. I'm home.
J: Hello, darling. How was work?
K: It was OK. What's for dinner?
J: Spaghetti.
K: Oh. OK. Can I turn on the TV?
J: Uh, yeah, sure.
4.
F: So, Jeff. How was your week?
J: It wasn't very good. My Aunt Dorothy is here, my son is . . .
F: Oh! What's the matter? Jeff, could you pass the milk?
J: Yeah, sure.

2.37 (Page 97)
Louise: My school was called Washington High School. It was in San Francisco. I was there from 1981 to 1986. It was a good school, but I wasn't a very good student. I was good at sports and art, but I was pretty bad at math and science and languages. My favorite class was art. My teacher was Mr. Little, and he was great. My best friend was Katie Wilson. She was in my class and she was a lot of fun!

UNIT 10 Past and future events

2.38 (Page 99)
1. You lose your wallet.
2. A thief steals your cell phone.
3. You stay in bed all day.
4. You win the lottery.
5. You get married.
6. You find $10 on the street.
7. A police officer arrests you.
8. You move to a new house.
9. You break your leg.
10. You meet your favorite actor.

2.40 (Page 101)
wanted /ɪd/; worked /t/; asked /t/; talked /t/; moved /d/; closed /d/; started /ɪd/; cooked /t/; finished /t/; arrested /ɪd/; lived /d/; walked /t/; played /d/; listened /d/

2.41 (Page 101)
The story of the Mona Lisa (Part 2)
The Mona Lisa **moved** to Versailles, and then to the Louvre. In 1800, Napoleon **moved** it to his bedroom, but it **didn't stay** there. Four years later, it was back in the Louvre.
Then, on August 21st, 1911, the Louvre **closed** its doors. There was a big problem. The Mona Lisa wasn't there! Who was the thief? The police **talked** to lots of people. They **talked** to Picasso. Was he the thief? He wasn't. But they **didn't talk** to Vincenzo Peruggia.

2.43 (Page 103)
It's Christmas in July at Discount Electronics! Come down to Discount Electronics today. We've got low, low prices on hundreds of items.

A fantastic DVD player was a hundred and ninety-nine dollars. Sale price: one hundred and forty-nine.

A great laptop computer was thirteen thirty-nine. Sale price: one thousand and fifteen!

A beautiful Kenroko washing machine was six hundred and twenty-five dollars. Sale price: four hundred and sixty-five!

Hurry. Sale ends soon.

A great 32-inch flat screen TV was one thousand eighty-nine dollars Sale price: seven hundred and fifty.

A new fridge was five-oh-five. Sale price: four twenty-seven!

And a fantastic Bilman stove was four hundred and sixty-nine dollars. Sale price: three hundred and twenty-five!

Remember, our sale ends tomorrow, so hurry on down to Discount Electronics today!

2.44 (Page 104)
A=Abby C=Charlie N=Nick H=Haley
A: Hi, everyone. Sorry I'm late.
C: No problem. Nice to see you.
A: You, too Charlie. Hi Haley. You look great.
H: You, too.
A: Thanks. Hi Nick.
N: Nice to see you, Abby.
A: So how was your week, Nick?
N: Well, it was pretty interesting. I talked to my manager on Tuesday, and he gave me some news.
A: What?
N: My company is going to move to Texas.
H: To Texas! What are you going to do?
N: I'm not going to move to Texas. I'm going to find a new job.
C: Well, I'm glad you're going to stay here.
N: Yeah, me, too. You know, I was bored in that job, so it's OK really. How was your week, Abby?
A: Awful. Someone stole my cell phone.
H: That's terrible. Where? When?
A: Yesterday morning. On the train I think.
N: Too bad. So did you get a new phone?
A: No, I'm so busy, there wasn't time. I'm going to get a new phone tomorrow.
C: My week was busy, too. Lauren and I moved to a new apartment on Monday.
N: Oh great. How is it?
C: It's OK, but we're not going to stay there long. We're going to buy a house next year. How about you Haley?
H: Well, my week was very exciting. Daniel asked me to marry him.
A: He asked you to marry him! That's great!
N: What did you say?
H: I said yes!
C: Wow! Congratulations!
A: That's really exciting. When are you going to get married?
H: Oh, next year, I think, maybe in the summer. And of course you're all going to come to the wedding, . . .

ENGLISH in Common 1B

Workbook

Jonathan Bygrave

Series Consultants
María Victoria Saumell and Sarah Louisa Birchley

ALWAYS LEARNING PEARSON

UNIT 6
All about you

LESSON 1

Vocabulary

1a Circle five adjectives in the word find. Then complete the words below.

s	h	o	r	t
b	s	a	i	h
o	l	d	c	i
m	l	u	h	n
h	a	p	p	y

1. s *h o r t* 3. o ___ ___ 5. t ___ ___ ___
2. r ___ ___ ___ 4. h ___ ___ ___ ___

b Write the opposite words.

1. tall ________ 4. poor ________
2. unhappy ________ 5. young ________
3. heavy ________

2 Label the pictures with adjectives from Exercise 1.

1  *short*

2  ________

3  ________

4  ________

5  ________

6  ________

7  ________

8  ________

9  ________

10  ________

Grammar

3a Use the cues to make sentences with *I like* or *I don't like*.

1. (☺/coffee)
   I like coffee.
2. (☹/museums)
   I don't like museums.
3. (☺/rap music)
   ________.
4. (☹/soccer)
   ________.
5. (☺/computers)
   ________.
6. (☹/Indian food)
   ________.
7. (☹/tea)
   ________.
8. (☺/children)
   ________.
9. (☺/James Bond films)
   ________.
10. (☹/my manager)
   ________.

b Write questions and answers about the words in **bold**.

1. A: *Do you like coffee*? **coffee**
   B: Yes, *I do*.
2. A: *Do you like the countryside*? **the countryside**
   B: No, *I don't*.
3. A: ________? **Chinese food**
   B: Yes, ________.
4. A: ________? **modern buildings**
   B: No, ________.
5. A: ________? **salad**
   B: Yes, ________.
6. A: ________? **German cars**
   B: No, ________.
7. A: ________? **Harry Potter**
   B: Yes, ________.
8. A: ________? **The Beatles**
   B: No, ________.

Grammar

4a Replace the underlined words with object pronouns: *me, you, him, her, it, us,* or *them.*

Now that I'm 70 . . .

by Harold Parks

Now that I'm 70, I am happy. I have a lot of best friends. My children are my best friends. I like my children (1.). My sister is my best friend—I like my sister (2.). My brother is my best friend. I like my brother (3.). The television is my best friend. We are together every evening. I like the television (4.). And you are my best friend. I like you (5.). Do you like Harold Parks (6.)?

1. *them*
2. ______
3. ______
4. ______
5. ______
6. ______

b Replace the underlined words with the object pronouns or subject pronouns.

1. You and I are rich. *We*
2. They like you and me. ______
3. Kevin and Carrie are engineers. ______
4. Do you like Kevin and Carrie? ______
5. Ella Fitzgerald is my favorite singer. ______
6. I like Ella Fitzgerald. ______
7. Richard is my best friend. ______
8. I like Richard. ______

Reading

5 Read the answers. Match the questions from the box to the answers. One question will be used twice.

> Do you like big cities?
> Do you like vacations on the coast?
> Who are your favorite actors?
> What are your favorite things in life?
> Do you like pop music?

1. *Do you like pop music?*

Yes, I do—some of it. I like Christina Aguilera and Katie Perry—they're great.

2. ______

That's easy: Javier Bardem, Halle Berry, and Susan Sarandon. Javier Bardem is great in *Biutiful*. It's a really good film.

Kimberley

Micaela

3. ______

Yes, I do. Paris, Buenos Aires, and Kyoto are my favorites. Buenos Aires is fantastic.

4. ______

I like French films, chocolate, coffee from Africa, the color brown, and Italian fashion, for example, Versace.

5. ______

No, I don't, but I like vacations in the countryside. I think beach vacations are awful, but a vacation in, for example, the Rocky Mountains in the US, now that's great.

6. ______

That's a good question. I like Sunday mornings in bed, my friends, and family and . . . a good book.

Peter

LESSON 2

Vocabulary

1 Look at the pictures. Complete the sentences.

1. Fashion *designers* design clothes.

2. __________ cook food.

3. __________ build buildings.

4. __________ sell things.

5. __________ write articles.

6. __________ design buildings.

Grammar

2 Look at the chart. Complete Grace's sentences.

	Grace and Marlon	Steve and Shena
1. like their job	YES	NO
2. work in an office	YES	NO
3. sell cars	NO	YES
4. design buildings	YES	NO

1. Grace: *We like our jobs*. *They don't like their jobs*.
2. Grace: __________. __________.
3. Grace: __________. __________.
4. Grace: __________. __________.

3 Look at the magazine pictures. Complete the interview.

WEEKEND HOUSE SWAP

Two couples swap houses for a weekend and decorate!

Reporter: So, Sara and Mark, what do you *do* (1.)?

Sara: __________ (2.) fashion designers.

Reporter: And what about Pete and Nancy. What __________ (3.) they do?

Mark: __________ (4.) sales reps.

Reporter: What do Pete and Nancy __________ (5.)?

Sara: They like the coast and the countryside. __________ (6.) like blues and greens in their house. They like boats and rivers, but they __________ (7.) like cities, and they don't __________ (8.) black.

Reporter: __________ (9.) do you like? Do __________ (10.) like blues and greens in your house?

Mark: No, we __________ (11.). We like white. We like cities and towns. We __________ (12.) the countryside and the coast, too, but just for a weekend.

Reporter: OK, thanks. Happy decorating!

4a Complete the questions.

1. What ___*do*___ you design?
2. ________ do you do?
3. Where ________ you live?
4. ________ do you work for?
5. ________ do you work?

b Complete the conversation with the questions from Exercise 4a.

Neil: Excuse me. Kate, this is Lance.
Kate: Hello, Lance. Nice to meet you.
Lance: Nice to meet you, too.
Kate: ___*What do you do*___ (1.)?
Lance: I'm a fashion designer.
Kate: Oh really? ________ (2.)?
Lance: It's a company called Confident Designs.
Kate: ________ (3.)?
Lance: I design shoes and clothes.
Kate: Great! ________ (4.)?
Lance: In a small office in Brooklyn.
Kate: ________ (5.)?
Lance: In a house on Long Island. What do you do?

Communication

5a Complete the conversation with the words from the box.

articles	do	~~Great!~~	Oh really?
Where	Who	What	sales rep

Jose: How is your food?
Marta: ___*Great!*___ (1.) And this restaurant is beautiful.
Jose: Thanks. And you, sir?
Ricardo: Great, thank you. ________ (2.) is the chef?
Jose: I am.
Ricardo: ________ (3.)
Jose: Really. I'm glad you like the food. . . . Is this your first time in New York?
Ricardo: No, no. My wife and I come here a lot, for work.
Jose: ________ (4.) do you do?
Marta: I'm a ________ (5.) for a coffee machine company. I sell machines to restaurants and coffee shops—those kinds of places. And my husband is a reporter.
Ricardo: I write travel ________ (6.) for magazines—about US vacation places.
Jose: ________ (7.) do you live?
Marta: In Miami, Florida. What about you—Where ________ (8.) you come from?
Jose: Brazil. But now New York is my home.

b What are the people's occupations?

Jose: ________
Ricardo: ________
Marta: ________

LESSON 3

Vocabulary

1a Match the verbs to the nouns. One noun will be used more than once.

_d_	1. watch	a. to bed
____	2. start	b. up
____	3. eat	c. work
____	4. finish	~~d. TV~~
____	5. go	e. shower
____	6. get	f. a sandwich
____	7. take a	

b Match the phrases in Exercise 1a to the pictures.

1 _get up_

2 ____________

3 ____________

4 ____________

5 ____________

6 ____________

7 ____________

Grammar

2 Look at the pictures in Exercise 1b. Write sentences.

1. _She gets up at 10:30_ .
2. ____________ .
3. ____________ .
4. ____________ .
5. ____________ .
6. ____________ .
7. ____________ .

3 Read the description. Answer the questions.

1. Does Mrs. Moody start work early?
   Yes, she does .
2. Does she eat breakfast?
   ____________ .
3. Does she drink coffee?
   ____________ .
4. Does she go to the restaurant for lunch?
   ____________ .
5. Does she finish work late?
   ____________ .
6. Does she have any friends?
   ____________ .

My manager is Mrs. Moody. She starts work at seven o'clock every morning. She doesn't eat breakfast. She has a coffee at eleven o'clock. She has salad for lunch. She doesn't go to a restaurant—she eats her salad at her desk. She finishes work at about eight o'clock. She doesn't have any friends.

4 Use the cues to write complete sentences.

1. (I/like/salad)
   I like salad.
2. (Cheryl/finish/her English class/ten thirty)
   Cheryl finishes her English class at ten thirty.
3. (They/work/in a restaurant)
   ______.
4. (Hilary and Ben/not/eat fast food)
   ______.
5. (Connor/not/eat salad)
   ______.
6. (you/go to bed early?)
   ______.
7. (Uma/like/me?)
   ______.
8. (What/she/do?)
   ______.

Communication

5 Read Ina's story. Then complete the chart.
✓ = like/love; ✗ = don't/doesn't like.

	Ina	Billy	Bianca	Larry and Mel
Ina		✓		
Billy				
Bianca				
Larry and Mel				

Ina

So . . . my family is a bit strange. There's my husband, Billy, my best friend, Bianca, and my parents, Larry and Mel. Now I love Billy, of course, and Billy loves me. But Billy doesn't like Bianca. I don't know why, but he doesn't. And Bianca doesn't like him. She likes my parents, and they like her, but they don't like Billy. And, you know what, Billy doesn't like them. Now, of course, I like Bianca and my parents, and they all like me. But Billy isn't popular.

Writing

6 Complete the letter with the phrases from the box.

> How are you?
> and my team likes me.
> ~~89 Oak Street,~~
> Dear Stephen,
> Please write and tell me your news.
> Best wishes,
> December 2

Apartment 15
89 Oak Street (1.)
Cleveland, OH

______ (2.)

______ (3.)

______ (4.) I hope you're well.

I have a new job: I'm still with Copy Fast, but I'm a manager now. I get up early, and I work late. But I like my job ______ (5.).

David, the old manager, is a sales rep now. He works for a small company. He doesn't like his new job. He starts work early, and he drives all over the country.

______ (6.)
______ (7.)
Gary

UNITS 4–6 Review

There is/are

1 Complete the conversation with *there's, there is, there isn't, there are, there aren't, Is there,* or *Are there.*

1. A: Good morning. *Is there* (1.) a bank near here?
   B: Yes, ______ (2.). It's on Parliament Street.
   A: And ______ (3.) any museums near here?
   B: Yes, ______ (4.). ______ (5.) a small museum on Baker Street, and ______ (6.) a big museum across from the train station.
2. C: Hello. ______ (7.) any good restaurants in town?
   D: Yes, ______ (8.). ______ (9.) a good Japanese restaurant on Gatson Street, and ______ (10.) two good Mexican restaurants on Mile Road.
   C: Great. And ______ (11.) an ATM in this hotel?
   D: No, ______ (12.).

this/that/these/those

2 Circle the correct word.

1. *Those/This/These* is my brother. (*This* circled)
2. Who are *that/this/those* people over there?
3. How much is *that/these/those* hat?
4. Is *this/those/these* your camera?
5. *That/These/This* are my favorite stores.
6. This blue skirt is $19.99, and *those/that/this* red skirts are $21.99.
7. Can I have *those/these/that* white bag, please?
8. Are *that/these/this* shoes from Italy?

Object pronouns

3 Complete the sentences with *me, you, him, her, it, us,* or *them.*

1. He's my best friend. I really like *him*.
2. You're my brother but I don't like ______.
3. They're great. We like ______.
4. It's an ugly city. I don't like ______.
5. I'm very happy. She loves ______.
6. She's my manager. I don't like ______.
7. We like them, and they like ______.

Simple present

4 Complete the sentences with the verbs in parentheses. Use the simple present.

1. Gary is a chef. He *cooks* (cook) Italian food in a restaurant.
2. My parents *don't get up* (not get up) late.
3. I ______ (like) British pop music.
4. We're fashion designers. We ______ (design) shoes.
5. Sophie ______ (not eat) meat.
6. Miguel ______ (eat) a lot of salad.
7. Alex ______ (not like) soccer.
8. You ______ (finish) work late.
9. We are reporters. We ______ (write) newspaper articles.
10. Brian and Tara ______ (watch) TV in the evening.
11. Harry's sister ______ (love) your house.
12. Du-Ho ______ (start) work at ten o'clock.

5 Write questions and answers with the cues.

1. (Hyun Ok/eat a lot) (yes)
   A: *Does Hyun Ok eat a lot?* ? B: *Yes, she does.* .
2. (your sisters/like your wife) (no)
   A: ______? B: ______.
3. (you/play tennis) (yes)
   A: ______? B: ______.
4. (they/sell houses) (yes)
   A: ______? B: ______.
5. (Javier/love her) (no)
   A: ______? B: ______.
6. (your friends/live in Barcelona) (yes)
   A: ______? B: ______.
7. (Craig/eat fast food) (no)
   A: ______? B: ______.
8. (we/have any food in the house) (no)
   A: ______? B: ______.
9. (you/design clothes) (yes)
   A: ______? B: ______.

Time

6 Write the times in words.

1.  *three-forty-five*
2.  ____________
3.  ____________
4.  ____________
5.  ____________
6.  ____________
7.  ____________
8.  ____________

can/can't: ability

7 Put the words in order to make statements and questions.

1. daughter/Can/drive/your
   Can your daughter drive ____________?
2. can't/Steven/piano/the/play
   ____________.
3. Spanish/speak/They/can
   ____________.
4. you/a/use/Can/computer
   ____________?
5. dance/can/sing/and/Michelle
   ____________.
6. cook/husband/My/can't
   ____________.

can: requests

8 Complete the questions.

1. A: *How* *much* *are* (1.) the chicken salad sandwiches?
   B: They're $3.59.
   A: ______ ______ ______ (2.) an orange juice?
   B: It's $1.29.
   A: ______ ______ ______ ______ (3.) chicken salad sandwich and an orange juice, please?
   B: Certainly. Anything else?
   A: Yes. ______ ______ ______ ______ (4.) coffee, please?
2. C: ______ ______ ______ (5.) the cheese sandwiches?
   D: They're $3.29.
   C: ______ ______ ______ (6.) a piece of chocolate cake?
   D: It's $1.89.
   C: ______ ______ ______ ______ (7.) piece of chocolate cake, please?
   D: Certainly. Anything else?
   C: No, thank you.

Vocabulary

9 Use the cues to complete the sentences.

1. Do you like *Chinese* food? (China)
2. Renault is a(n) ____________ car company. (France)
3. Giorgio Armani is a(n) ____________ fashion designer. (Italy)
4. There are a lot of ____________ restaurants in the US. (Mexico)
5. Can you speak ____________? (Japan)
6. Younha is a famous ____________ singer. (Korea)

10 Match the verbs to the words or phrases.

f	1. use	a. an article
___	2. write	b. to bed
___	3. play	c. TV
___	4. design	d. dinner
___	5. finish	e. the piano
___	6. cook	~~f. a computer~~
___	7. go	g. work
___	8. watch	h. a building

UNIT 7
A day at work

LESSON 1

Vocabulary

1 Look at the pictures. Complete the crossword puzzle.

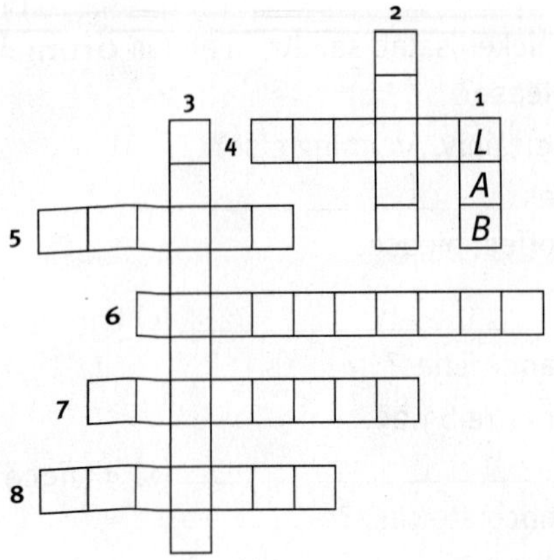

1 

2 

3 

4 

5 

6 

7 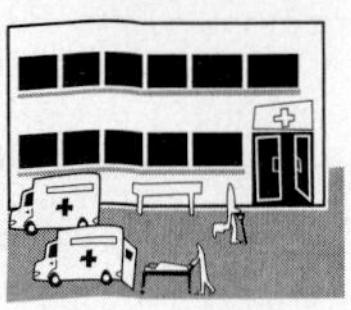

8 

2 Look at the pictures in Exercise 1 again. Write the places. Then write the jobs.

1. *lab* = *researcher*
2. ______ = ______
3. ______ = ______
4. ______ = ______
5. ______ = ______
6. ______ = ______
7. ______ = ______
8. ______ = ______

Grammar

3a Look at the pictures and use the cues to write imperatives.

1.  (quiet) *be quiet*

2.  (down) ______

3.  (hold) ______

4.  (look) ______

5.  (come) ______

b Write negative imperatives with the cues. Use *Please*.

1. (sit down) *Please don't sit down*.
2. (come in) ______.
3. (turn on your cell phone) ______.
4. (look at the next page) ______.
5. (watch TV) ______.

Communication

4 Complete the phone calls with the phrases from the box.

call back later	I'm sorry	It's
Good afternoon	Certainly	Hello
Hold on, please	How can I	Bye
Can I speak to		
take a message		

Conversation 1

Receptionist: Good morning. City Hospital.
Woman: Good morning. *Can I speak to* (1.) Andrew Holden, please?
Receptionist: Certainly. ______________ (2.). . .
Receptionist: Hello.
Woman: Hello.
Receptionist: ______________ (3.), but Mr. Holden is busy at the moment. Can I ______________ (4.)?
Woman: No, thank you. I can ______________ (5.).
Receptionist: OK. Thank you. Bye.
Woman: ______________ (6.).

Conversation 2

Receptionist: ______________ (7.) North Stone University.
Ted: Good afternoon. This is Ted Miller. Can I speak to Karen Long, please?
Receptionist: ______________ (8.) Hold on, please.
Karen: ______________ (9.), Karen Long speaking.
Ted: Hello, Karen. ______________ (10.) Ted.
Karen: Hello, Ted. How are you?
Ted: Fine, thanks. And you?
Karen: Not bad. Busy as always. ______________ (11.) help you?

Vocabulary

5a Complete the months. Then put them in order.

J *u* l y (7)
__ c t __ b __ r ( )
J __ n __ __ r y ( )
D __ c __ m b __ r ( )
__ __ g __ s t ( )
M __ y ( )
__ p r __ l ( )
F __ b r __ __ r __ ( )
N __ v __ m b __ r ( )
J __ n __ ( )
S __ p t __ m b __ r ( )
M __ r c h ( )

b Cover the months in Exercise 5a. Write the birthday months of the celebrities.

1. Maria Sharapova (04/19/1987) *April*
2. Giorgio Armani (07/11/1934) ______________
3. Roger Federer (08/08/1981) ______________
4. John Travolta (02/18/1954) ______________
5. Bruce Springsteen (09/23/1949) ______________
6. Bono (5/10/1960) ______________
7. Angelina Jolie (06/04/1975) ______________
8. Sting (10/02/1951) ______________
9. Brooklyn Beckham (03/04/1999) ______________

LESSON 2

Vocabulary

1a Circle the correct verb.

1. *work/call/write* customers
2. *answer/have/write* the phone
3. *work/travel/write* reports
4. *work/give/have* outdoors
5. *call/give/answer* presentations
6. *answer/travel/have* for work
7. *attend/write/work* meetings

b Write the verb phrases below the pictures.

A

travel for work

B

____

C

____

D

____

E

____

F

____

G

____

Grammar

2a Write the words from the box in the correct place.

often	never	usually	sometimes
not often/not usually			always

100% **a.** ________
b. ________
c. *often*
d. ________
e. ________
0% **f.** ________

b Put the words in the correct order to make sentences.

1. afternoon/watch/TV/never/I/in the
   I never watch TV in the afternoon.
2. work/Maggie/usually/home/doesn't/take
   ________________.
3. We/outdoors/work/sometimes
   ________________.
4. to/always/go/Do/bed/you/at eleven o'clock?
   ________________?
5. golf/He/Sundays/often/plays/on
   ________________.
6. for work/They/travel/don't often/
   ________________.

3 Rewrite the sentences with adverbs of frequency.

1. I swim in the ocean.
   (not often) *I don't often swim in the ocean*.
2. I'm late for work.
   (sometimes) ________________.
3. I drive.
   (never) ________________.
4. I sing and play the piano at family parties.
   (usually) ________________.
5. My manager answers the phone at work.
   (not usually) ________________.
6. He is happy on Friday afternoons.
   (always) ________________.

Reading

4a Read the three descriptions. Write the jobs. Then match the jobs to the people.

A

B

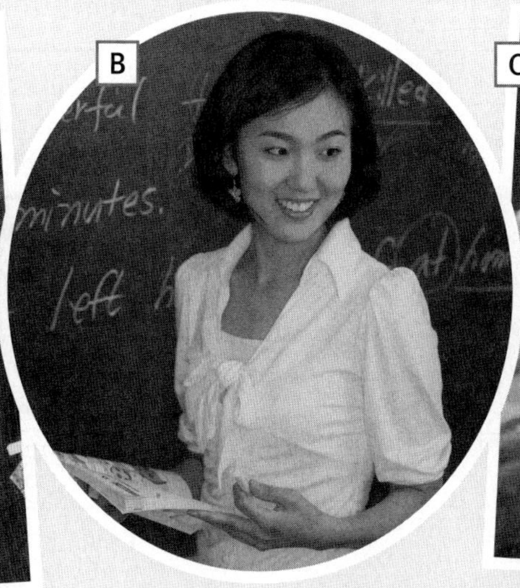

C

1. _____ Job: ______________

Regina doesn't work in an office. She talks to customers a lot but she doesn't usually call them. She always works on Saturdays. She doesn't give presentations or write reports, and she doesn't use a computer.

Regina: "I like my job. I always start work at nine and finish at five. I don't think about my job after five o'clock."

2. _____ Job: ______________

Darcy doesn't work in an office, and she doesn't work in a school. She sometimes starts work in the morning, sometimes in the afternoon, and sometimes at night. She often works on weekends. In Darcy's job there aren't any customers, but she talks to people every day.

Darcy: "I love my job. I like the doctors, but I don't like the nights."

3. _____ Job: ______________

Olivia doesn't work in a factory or a lab. She starts work at nine and finishes at five every day. She never works on weekends. She doesn't call customers, but she often sends emails to her students.

Olivia: "My job is OK. I don't love it and I don't hate it."

b Read the descriptions again. Complete the sentences with the names of the people.

1. *Olivia* never works on Saturday.
2. ______________ works at a university.
3. ______________ doesn't start work at nine o'clock every day.
4. ______________ and ______________ never call customers.
5. ______________ works in a store.
6. ______________ works in a hospital.
7. ______________ uses a computer at work.

Writing

5 Write a note with the phrases from the box.

Can you	call me at home	Laura
~~Hi Jared,~~	this afternoon?	Thanks,
My phone number	is 506-555-1312.	

Hi Jared,

Vocabulary

1a Complete the crossword puzzle.

Clues

Across

2. 4th
5. 30th
7. 11th
10. 19th
11. 8th
12. 3rd

Down

1. 5th
3. 12th
4. 15th
6. 20th
8. 1st
9. 2nd

b Write the dates using numbers.

1. January twenty-first *January 21, 1/21*
2. March eleventh ______
3. May first ______
4. December twelfth ______
5. June twentieth ______
6. November sixteenth ______
7. September second ______
8. February third ______

Grammar

2a Complete the conversation with the phrases from the box.

I'd like some	What would you like
thank you	~~What would you like to~~
I'd like	Would you like

A: Hello, Mr. Wallace. My name's Orla Birch.
B: Hello, Ms. Birch. This is Mrs. Trenter.
A: Nice to meet you, Mrs. Trenter.
C: Nice to meet you, too.
A: Please, come into my office. *What would you like to* (1.) drink?
B: ______ (2.) coffee, please.
C: And I'd like a cup of tea, please.
A: ______ (3.) milk and sugar?
B: No, ______ (4.).
C: Yes, please.
A: ______ (5.) something to eat? A piece of cake?
B: I'd like some fruit, please.
C: ______ (6.) a piece of cake. Thank you.

b Write questions and answers with the words in **bold**.

1. A: *Would you like a coffee*? **coffee**
   B: *No, thank you*. **No**
2. A: *What would you like to eat*? **to eat**
   B: *I'd like a sandwich, please*. **sandwich**
3. A: ______. **bottled water**
   B: ______. **No**
4. A: ______? **orange juice**
   B: ______. **Yes**
5. A: ______? **to drink**
   B: ______. **a cup of tea**
6. A: ______? **piece of cake**
   B: ______. **Yes**
7. A: ______? **to eat**
   B: ______. **a salad**
8. A: ______? **iced tea**
   B: ______. **No**

Vocabulary

3a Put the letters in order to make food words.

1. sgeetlvabe — *vegetables*
2. opsu — s__________
3. dlaas — s__________
4. kindrs — d__________
5. truif — f__________
6. sseertsd — d__________
7. sskcna — s__________
8. zprstraepie — a__________
9. acmisurone — m__________ c__________

b Complete the story with words from Exercise 3a.

When I go to a restaurant, I always have an  *appetizer* (1.), for example, chicken  __________ (2.) and I never have any  __________ (3.) before the meal.

For a  __________ (4.) I usually order an Italian dish, for example spaghetti bolognese with a  __________ (5.) or some fresh  __________ (6.).

I never have  __________ (7.), but sometimes I order a plate of fresh  __________ (8.). I don't have orange  __________ (9.)—just some bottled water.

Communication

4 Read the conversations. Then circle the correct picture for each conversation.

Conversation 1

A: What would you like?
B: I'd like vegetable soup, a salad, and chicken, please.
A: Here you are.
B: Thanks.

Conversation 2

A: Hello, Mr. Adams. Welcome to our factory.
B: Thank you.
A: Would you like a coffee?
B: Yes, please. With milk and sugar, please.

Conversation 3

A: OK, before the meeting, what would you like to drink?
B: Can I have a cup of tea, please?
A: Sure. Would you like a piece of cake?
B: Yes, please.
A: Chocolate cake?
B: Great.

Conversation 1

A

B

Conversation 2

C

D

Conversation 3

E

F

UNIT 8

Your likes and dislikes

LESSON 1

Vocabulary

1a Match the words in the box to the pictures.

TV	tennis	reading	swimming
eating	biking	soccer	sightseeing
~~chess~~	theater	hiking	working out

1.  *chess*
2.  ________
3.  ________
4.  ________
5.  ________
6.  ________
7.  ________
8.  ________
9.  ________
10.  ________
11.  ________
12.  ________

b Write verb phrases for the leisure activities in Exercise 1a.

1. *play chess*
2. ________
3. ________
4. ________
5. ________
6. ________
7. ________
8. ________
9. ________
10. ________
11. ________
12. ________

Communication

2 Look at the chart. Complete the conversation.

	Jeff's house	Jorge's house	Mika's house
	✓	✓	✓
	✓	✗	✓
	✗	✓	✗
	✗	✗	✓
	✗	✓	✗

A: Where do you want to go this weekend?

B: How about Jeff's house. *You* *can* *watch* (1.) TV and ________ ________ ________ (2.) chess at his house.

A: Yeah, but I want to work out. What about Jorge's house? ________ ________ ________ (3.) tennis and ________ ________ (4.).

B: But I want to swim. How about Mika's house. ________ ________ ________ (5.) swimming at her house. She has a swimming pool.

A: Good idea.

Grammar

3 Complete the sentences with *want* or *like*.

1. Marcus and Pete *want* to play soccer.
2. Do you ________ to go out to eat?
3. Which restaurant do you ________ to go to?
4. They don't ________ watching TV.
5. Does she ________ playing tennis?
6. Do you ________ hiking?
7. I don't ________ playing chess.
8. We ________ to go to the theater.

4 Complete the stories with the verbs in parentheses.

My name is Kate Watson. I'm a chef. I work for a small restaurant called The Happy Chicken. I like *being* (1. be) a chef, and I like ________ (2. work) with food. But I don't like ________ (3. finish) work at one o'clock in the morning. I want ________ (4. work) from nine to five, and I want ________ (5. go) out with my friends in the evening. I never see my friends—I'm always at work!

My name is Johan Holland. I'm a construction worker. I like ________ (6. build) things, but I don't like my job. It's not exciting. I want ________ (7. be) a sales rep. I like ________ (8. travel) for work and I like ________ (9. sell) things. I don't want ________ (10. build) things for eight hours a day.

Vocabulary

5a Rearrange the letters to make adjectives.

1. iiucfdftl = d*ifficult*
2. yase = e________
3. igrobn = b________
4. nuf = f________
5. netgixic = e________
6. sirtintegne = i________

b Complete the sentences with the adjectives from Exercise 5a.

1. I got 3 out of 20 points on my math test. Math is very *difficult* for me.
   Ed Moller, 16, student
2. I can speak Japanese, English, and Spanish. Languages are very ________ for me.
   Asenka Chazov, 14, student
3. I read two or three books every week. Books are very ________.
   Armina Lang, 49, lecturer
4. I don't like having meetings at work. I want to sleep in meetings. They're ________.
   Uri Anderson, 42, sales manager
5. I like traveling and meeting new people. It's ________.
   Dan Adams, 26, reporter
6. I go out with friends from work every Friday evening. It's ________.
   Josie West, fashion designer

Writing

6 Read the ad. Then complete the email to the hotel.

Mountain View Hotel

A beautiful hotel in the heart of the Big Sky country.

- 6 double rooms
- 2 single rooms
- heated swimming pool
- much more!

Come to Mountain View Hotel for a weekend away or a vacation!

mountainviewhotel@montana.net

bikes, too???

breakfast included???

From: kenchang@worldwidemail.com

To: *mountainviewhotel@montana.net* (1.)

Subject: room for December 18–19

Dear ________ (2.)

I ________ (3.) some more information about your hotel.

- Do you have a ________ (4.) room available for my wife and me on ________ (5.)?
- ________ (6.) is it for two nights?
- Is breakfast ________ (7.)?
- Does the hotel have ________ (8.)?

I ________ (9.) to your reply.

Yours ________ (10.),

Ken Chang

LESSON 2

Vocabulary

1a Match furniture words from the box to the pictures.

~~sofa~~	fridge	armchair	dishwasher
car	stove	cabinet	coffee table
bed	mirror	bathtub	
sink	toilet		

1 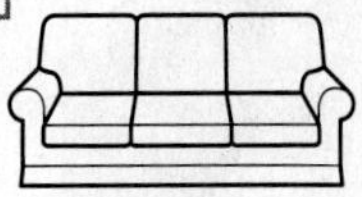
sofa

2 
______

3 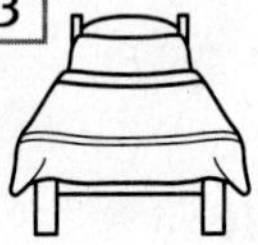
______

4 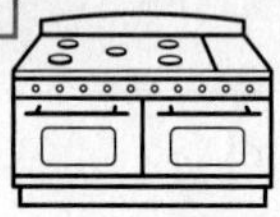
______

5 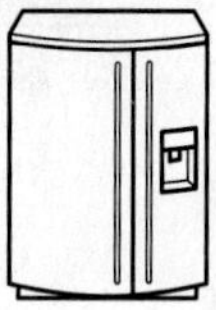
______

6 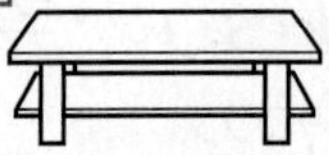
______

7 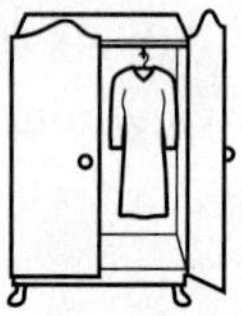
______

8 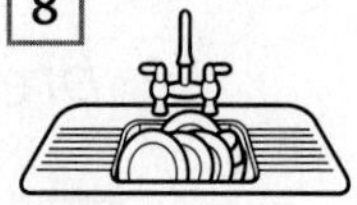
______

9 
______

10 
______

11 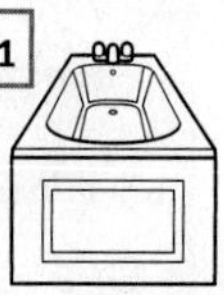
______

12 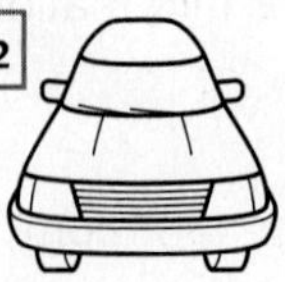
______

13 
______

b Match the furniture words in Exercise 1a to the rooms.

Bathroom: ______ ______

Bedroom: ______ ______ ______

Kitchen: ______ ______ ______ ______

Living room: *sofa* ______ ______

Garage: ______

Grammar

2a Look at the chart. Complete Jamie's story.

	Jamie	Patricia
bedrooms	1	2
garage	✗	✓
dishwasher	✓	✗
bathtub	✗	✓
sofa	✓	✓
car	✓	✗

I *have* (1.) a small apartment in Boston, USA. It ______ (2.) one bedroom and a living room. It ______ (3.) a garage. I ______ (4.) a dishwasher in the kitchen and a sofa in the living room. I ______ (5.) a bathtub—just a shower. I ______ (6.) a car—it's a small, red sports car.

b Look at the chart. Complete Patricia's story.

She *has* (1.) a house in Auckland, New Zealand. It ______ (2.) two bedrooms and a garage. She ______ (3.) a bathtub in the bathroom and a sofa in the living room. She ______ (4.) a dishwasher and she ______ (5.) a car.

3 Complete the conversation.

A: Hello. Can I help you?

B: No, thank you. I'm just looking.

A: Our TVs are on sale today. *Do* you *have* (1.) a TV?

B: Yes, I ______ (2.).

A: ______ you ______ (3.) a TV in your bedroom?

B: No, I ______ (4.). But I don't want a TV. I want a dishwasher for my mother.

A: ______ your mother ______ (5.) a TV in her bedroom?

B: Yes, she ______ (6.). Now, how much is this dishwasher?

A: It's $399. The TV is only $299 . . .

4 Use the cues to write sentences with *have, has, do,* and *does.*

1. (you/a car) (✓)
   A: *Do you have a car* ?
   B: *Yes, I do* .
2. (Ravi/a new house) (✓)
   Ravi has a new house .
3. (My parents/a dishwasher) (✗)
   ______________________.
4. (your house/a garage) (✗)
   A: ______________________?
   B: ______________________.
5. (that hotel/a swimming pool) (✓)
   A: ______________________?
   B: ______________________.
6. (my hotel room/bathtub) (✗)
   ______________________.
7. (we/a new baby) (✓)
   ______________________.
8. (you/a beautiful house) (✓)
   ______________________.
9. (my sisters/any children) (✗)
   ______________________.
10. (we/any milk in the fridge) (✓)
    A: ______________________?
    B: ______________________.
11. (you/an extra pencil) (✗)
    A: ______________________?
    B: ______________________.
12. (they/a son named Fred) (✓)
    A: ______________________?
    B: ______________________.

Reading

5 Read about Jason and answer the questions.

I want to live in . . .

This week we talk to university professor and writer Jason Thomas.

I want to live In Cuzco in Peru. It's not the capital of Peru, but it's Peru's oldest city. It's interesting and exciting. I love it.

Cuzco is in the south of Peru. It's 800 years old! It has a lot of hotels, stores, and restaurants. My favorite place is the ruins (old city and buildings) of Machu Picchu. It's amazing.

My friends live in Cuzco, and they have a nice house near the center of the city. They also have a small house in the mountains for weekends and vacations.

1. Is Cuzco the capital of Peru?
   No, it isn't .
2. How old is it?
   ______________________.
3. What is Jason's favorite place?
   ______________________.
4. What is Machu Picchu?
   ______________________.
5. Where do Jason's friends go for weekends and vacations?
   ______________________.

Communication

1 Complete the conversation with *What about . . . ?* or *How about . . . ?* and phrases from the box.

a swim in the lake
a game of chess
that new coffee shop on Baker Street
seeing a movie
~~playing tennis~~

A: What do you want to do this afternoon?
B: *How about playing tennis* ? (1.)
A: No. I don't like tennis.
B: ______________________ ? (2.)
A: No. I don't like swimming.
B: ______________________ ? (3.)
A: No. I don't want to go to a coffee shop.
B: ______________________ ? (4.)
A: No. I can't play chess.
B: ______________________ ? (5.)
A: Good idea. Which movie?

Grammar

2 Complete the questions with question words.

1. A: *What* do you teach?
   B: I teach English.
2. A: ________ is your favorite actor?
   B: Jean Claude Van Damme.
3. A: ________ far is your school?
   B: It's about 2 blocks from here.
4. A: ________ is Jackie?
   B: She's in the bathroom.
5. A: ________ Elvis song is this?
   B: It's "You Are Always on my Mind."
6. A: ________ is your teacher?
   B: Mrs. Malkmus.
7. A: ________ table do you like?
   B: I like this table. It's nice.

3 Read the descriptions. Then write a question for each answer.

Kathleen Stock is a university professor from Cork, Ireland. She's 42 years old, and she works for Dublin City University. Her husband is Tom Stock.

1. Q: *What is her last name* ?
   A: Stock.
2. Q: ________________ ?
   A: She's a university professor.
3. Q: ________________ ?
   A: Cork, Ireland.
4. Q: ________________ ?
   A: forty-two.
5. Q: ________________ ?
   A: Dublin City University.
6. Q: ________________ ?
   A: He's her husband.

Iznik is a small restaurant in Denver, Colorado. It serves excellent Turkish food. A typical meal costs $15. The owner is a woman named Ceylan Yildirim. She's from Bodrum in Turkey.

7. Q: ________________ ?
   A: Iznik.
8. Q: ________________ ?
   A: Turkish food.
9. Q: ________________ ?
   A: Denver, Colorado.
10. Q: ________________ ?
    A: $15
11. Q: ________________ ?
    A: Ceylan Yildirim
12. Q: ________________ ?
    A: Bodrum in Turkey.

Communication

4 Complete the conversations.

Conversation 1

Waiter: Hello. Gino's restaurant.

Sam: Hello. I'd *like* (1.) to reserve a table for Saturday evening.

Waiter: Certainly. ________ (2.) many people?

Sam: Two.

Waiter: What ________ (3.)?

Sam: Nine o'clock, please.

Waiter: And what's the name, please?

Sam: Sam Allman.

Waiter: OK. ________ (4.) you on Saturday.

Sam: Thank you. Good-bye.

Conversation 2

Waiter: Hello. Do you have a ________ (1.)?

Sam: Yes, we do. My name's Sam Allman.

Waiter: A(n) ________ (2.) for two?

Sam: Yes, that's right.

Waiter: ________ (3.) with me, please.

Waiter: Are you ________ (4.) to order?

Sam: Yes. I'd ________ (5.) chicken soup, please, and lamb chops.

Waiter: Certainly. And for you ma'am?

Tara: Can I ________ (6.) seafood pasta, please? No appetizer, thank you.

Waiter: Certainly. What would you like to ________ (7.)?

Sam: Can I have an orange juice, please?

Tara: And I'd like some bottled water, please.

(*later*)

Sam: Excuse me. Can I have the ________ (8.), please?

Waiter: Of course.

Vocabulary

5 Look at the pictures. Complete the puzzle to find the secret phrase.

UNIT 9
Your life

LESSON 1

Vocabulary

1 Correct the phrases.

Write	Say
1. 1982	nineteen and eighty-two *nineteen eighty-two*
2. 2009	two hundred and nine __________
3. 1803	eighteen zero three __________
4. 1909	nineteen hundred and nine __________
5. 1970	nineteen seventeen __________

2 Read the "Fun Facts" article. Then write the details next to the pictures.

Fun Facts!

- The first TV ad was on July 1, 1941. It was ten seconds long, and it cost just nine dollars.
- The first newspaper crossword was on December 21, 1913. It was called a "Word-cross."
- The first cell phone call was on April 3, 1973. It was in New York.
- The first tourist in space was on April 28, 2001. His name was Dennis Tito.

1. 

July 1, 1941
ten seconds
long, $9

2. 
____
____

3. 
____
____

4. 
____
____

Grammar

3 Complete the articles with *was* or *were*.

Peter Sellers was a British icon. He *was* (1.) born on September 8, 1925, in Hampshire in the UK. His parents __________ (2.) Agnes and Bill Sellers. They __________ (3.) actors and singers in the theater. In the 1950s, Peter Sellers __________ (4.) a radio star. In the 1960s and 1970s he __________ (5.) a movie star. *The Pink Panther* and *Dr. Strangelove* __________ (6.) some of Peter Sellers' movies.

John, Paul, George, and Ringo __________ (7.) The Beatles. They __________ (8.) from Liverpool in the UK. The band's first name __________ (9.) The Quarrymen. In 1961 they __________ (10.) popular in Liverpool and Hamburg, Germany. Their first hit, in 1962, __________ (11.) "Love Me Do." Their next song, "Please Please Me," __________ (12.) number one in early 1963. *Revolver* and *Let It Be* __________ (13.) some of the albums by the Beatles.

4 Rewrite the sentences with *was* or *were*.

1. Jeff and I are late for the party.
Jeff and I were late for the party.
2. My son and daughter are at home.
__________.
3. I'm a computer engineer.
__________.
4. You're my best friend.
__________.
5. We're in the garage.
__________.
6. Franz is my sister's best friend.
__________.
7. This book is really exciting.
__________.
8. She's a university professor in London.
__________.

Communication

5 Put the words in the correct order to make sentences.

1. good/When/young,/I was/actor./I was a
 When I was young, I was a good actor.
2. she was a/When/beautiful./she was/child,
 ____
3. children,/friends./When they/they were/were
 ____
4. was young,/When he/Tim/very thin./was
 ____
5. you/were you/a child,/When/were/happy?
 ____
6. I was/wasn't/young,/good at/When/I/sports.
 ____

Vocabulary

6 Use the cues and the words from the box to write sentences.

in	at	of	~~on~~	for	with

1. (Einstein/born/March 14, 1879)
 Einstein was born on March 14, 1879.
2. (Alfred Hitchcock/famous/his movies)
 ____________________.
3. (Margaret Thatcher/friends/Ronald Reagan)
 ____________________.
4. (Martin Luther King Jr. and Spike Lee/born/Atlanta in Georgia)
 ____________________.
5. (Lyndon Johnson/president/the US/ from 1963 to 1969)
 ____________________.
6. (Lola Beltrán/good/singing)
 ____________________.

Reading

7 Read the webpage. Then mark the statements true (*T*) or false (*F*).

____ 1. Franklin D. Roosevelt was the first American to win the Nobel Peace Prize.
____ 2. The first American to win the Nobel Prize for peace was Theodore Roosevelt.
____ 3. John D. Rockefeller was a billionaire in the UK.
____ 4. The first World Cup was in Argentina.
____ 5. The first World Cup winner was Uruguay.

http://www.famousfirsts.com/

More Famous Firsts

1st

You ask the questions, we find the answers!

Which president was the first American to win the Nobel Peace Prize? *Polly Harris*

Well, Polly, the first American to win the Nobel Prize for his efforts to create world peace was Theodore Roosevelt.

Who was the first billionaire? *Jing Xu*

Good question, Jing. The first billionaire in American money was John D. Rockefeller in 1916. His company was Standard Oil.

When was the first World Cup? *Marta Diaz*

The first World Cup was in 1930 in Uruguay. There were 13 countries in the competition. Argentina and Uruguay were the two teams in the final. Uruguay was the winner, 4–2.

Grammar

1a Read the profile. Then use the cues to write sentences.

Cate Blanchett

PROFILE

Name: Catherine Elise Blanchett
Born: May 14, 1969, in Melbourne, Australia
Father: Robert Blanchett, from the US
Mother: June Blanchett, from Australia
Childhood: good actor in high school
University: Melbourne University (economics)
First big film: *Oscar and Lucinda*
Children: Dashiell (born 2001), Roman (born 2004), Ignatius (born 2008)

1. (Cate/born/the US)
   Cate wasn't born in the US .
   She was born in Australia .
2. (Her father/from/the UK)
   ________ .
   ________ .
3. (She/a good singer/at school)
   ________ .
   ________ .
4. (Her major in school/English)
   ________ .
   ________ .
5. (Her first big movie/*Elizabeth I*)
   ________ .
   ________ .
6. (Her children/born/2002, 2003, 2005)
   ________ .
   ________ .

b Write questions with the cues in Exercise 1a. Then write the answers.

1. *Was Cate born in the US* ?
   No she wasn't .
2. ________ ?
   ________ .
3. ________ ?
   ________ .
4. ________ ?
   ________ .
5. ________ ?
   ________ .
6. ________ ?
   ________ .

2 Complete the conversation with *was, wasn't, were,* or *weren't.*

Interviewer: So, Melissa, when you *were* (1.) a child, ________ (2.) you a good singer?
Melissa: No, I ________ (3.). I ________ (4.) a very bad singer.
Interviewer: Who ________ (5.) your singing teacher?
Melissa: Her name ________ (6.) Mrs. Parsons. She ________ (7.) great—really great!
Interviewer: Who ________ (8.) your favorite singers?
Melissa: Aretha Franklin and Billie Holiday ________ (9.) my favorite singers.
Interviewer: ________ (10.) your parents singers?
Melissa: No, they ________ (11.). My mother ________ (12.) a scientist, and my father ________ (13.) a sales rep.

3 Correct the mistakes.

1. Was you a good singer when you were young?
   Were you a good singer when you were young ?
2. Richard and Alex isn't at work yesterday.
   ________ .
3. I not a math teacher. I was a science teacher.
   ________ .
4. Were Ronald Reagan a movie star?
   ________ .
5. My father not a composer, but he was a musician.
   ________ .
6. Was you at home last night?
   ________ .
7. When were your last vacation?
   ________ .
8. Who your best friend was at school?
   ________ .
9. What were Marlon Brando's last movie?
   ________ .

Vocabulary

4a Read the blog post. Then put the pictures in time order.

> My name is Keiko Tagawa. I work for Trans-Global Software. I travel for work a lot. For example, last week I was in Moscow. Three days ago I was in Athens. Fifteen days ago I was in New York. Yesterday I was in London. Last month I was in Paris.

____ **A**

____ **B**

_1_ **C**

____ **D**

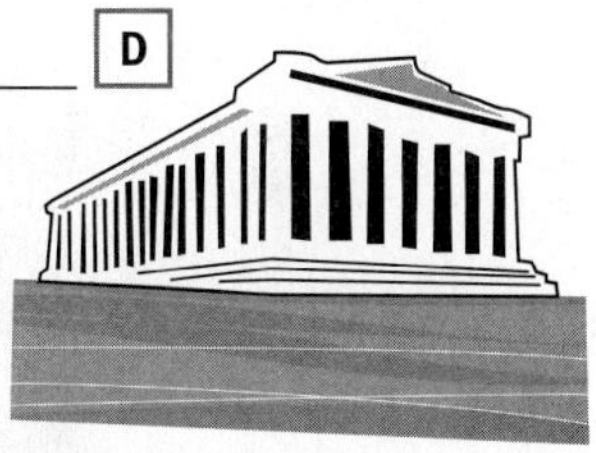

____ **E**

b Complete the phrases with *yesterday, ago,* or *last.*

Today is Wednesday March 24, 2011

1. March 23, evening = _yesterday_ _evening_
2. March 17 = ________ ________ ________
3. 2007 = ________ ________ ________
4. March 23, night = ________ night
5. Monday March 15 – Sunday March 21 = ________ ________
6. March 14 = ten ________ ________
7. February 2011 = ________ ________
8. March 23 morning = ________ ________

Communication

5a Complete the conversation with the words from the box. Some words are used twice.

Would	~~right~~	was
wasn't	that	

A: Hello. Are you Mr. Sarandon?
B: Yes, that's _right_ (**1.**).
A: I'm Marianne. Nice to meet you.
B: Hello, Marianne. Nice to meet you, too. Please, sit down. ________ (**2.**) you like some coffee?
A: No, thank you.
B: So, you want a job in The Coffee Palace.
A: Yes, that's right.
B: What ________ (**3.**) your last job?
A: I was a sales clerk in a department store.
B: Was that here in Chicago?
A: No, it ________ (**4.**). It was in San Diego. I'm from California.
B: I see. What was the name of the store?
A: Favorite Fashions.
B: Was ________ (**5.**) your first job after high school?
A: No, it wasn't. My first job was in a research lab. That ________ (**6.**) very interesting. It was boring.
B: OK. Can you make good coffee?
A: I can make great coffee . . .

b Read the conversation again. Then answer the questions.

1. What does Marianne want?
   ________________.
2. Where is The Coffee Palace?
   ________________.
3. What was Marianne's last job?
   ________________.
4. What is Favorite Fashions?
   ________________.
5. Where was Marianne's first job after high school?
   ________________.
6. Can she make good coffee?
   ________________.

LESSON 3

Vocabulary

1a Choose the correct word.

1. *cook/iron/wash* dinner
2. *wash/clean/do* the laundry
3. *iron/vacuum/cook* the house
4. *cook/wash/clean* the bathroom
5. *iron/cook/vacuum* a shirt
6. *cook/iron/wash* the dishes

b Write housework words from Exercise 1a below the pictures.

A

iron a shirt

B

______

C

______

D

______

E

______

F

______

Communication

2 Complete the conversations with questions from the box.

~~How was your flight?~~	How was school?
How was your weekend?	How was the party?
How was your vacation?	

1. A: *How was your flight?*
   B: It was OK, but the flight attendants weren't very nice.
2. A: ______
   B: It was good. My teacher likes me!
3. A: ______
   B: It was great. There were 50 people there.
4. A: ______
   B: Fine, thanks. I was in town on Saturday, and I was at home on Sunday.
5. A: ______
   B: It was great. The weather was beautiful, and the food was very nice.

Grammar

3 Match the conversations to the pictures.

1. A: Could you carry my suitcase?
   B: Of course.
2. A: Can I use your phone?
   B: Yes, you can.
3. A: Could I have a cup of tea?
   B: Yes, of course.
4. A: Could you take a photo of us?
   B: Yes, sure.
5. A: Could you answer the phone?
   B: Yes, OK.

______ A

______ B

1 C

______ D

______ E

4 Put the words in the correct order to make requests and ask for permission.

1. you/I/to/Can/talk
   Can I talk to you ?
2. you/dinner/Can/cook
   ______?
3. the/Could/open/you/window
   ______?
4. down/I/Can/sit
   ______?
5. on that report/work/I/tomorrow/Could
   ______?
6. on/TV/Could/turn/you/the
   ______?
7. help/I/with/you/that/Could
   ______?
8. out/I/Can/go/tonight
   ______?

5 Write a suggestion. Use *Could you . . . ?* and phrases from Exercise 1a.

1. A: *Could you iron my shirts* ?
   B: Sorry, I can't. The iron is broken.
2. A: ______?
   B: Sorry, I can't. The washing machine is broken.
3. A: ______?
   B: Sure. What would you like to eat?
4. A: ______?
   B: Yes, OK. Where's the vacuum cleaner?
5. A: ______?
   B: I can't. The kitchen sink is broken.
6. A: ______?
   B: I can't. My brother is taking a shower!

Writing

6 Read the letter. Find and correct nine mistakes.

Dear Tesia,

Long time ~~not~~ no see. How are you?

Thanks for your last letter. How were your vacation? Our vacation wasn't very good. The hotel was awful, and the weather is very bad.

My family fine, thank you. Viktor is four, and Roza is two year old now. I have a new job. Last year I'm a sales rep, but now I'm a sales manager. The new job is exciting, but I work long hours.

There is a conference in your city next Thursday. I could stay at your house on Wednesday night? I can stay in a hotel, but I want see you.

Could send me an email or call me this week?

Love,

Joanna

UNIT 10
Past and future events

LESSON 1

Vocabulary

1a Complete the sentences. Then write the verbs in the puzzle to find the secret phrase.

1. You *win* the lottery.
2. You ____________ some money on the street.
3. You ____________ a famous person.
4. A police officer ____________ you.
5. You ____________ to a new house.
6. You ____________ your leg.
7. A thief ____________ your cell phone.
8. You ____________ your wallet or purse.

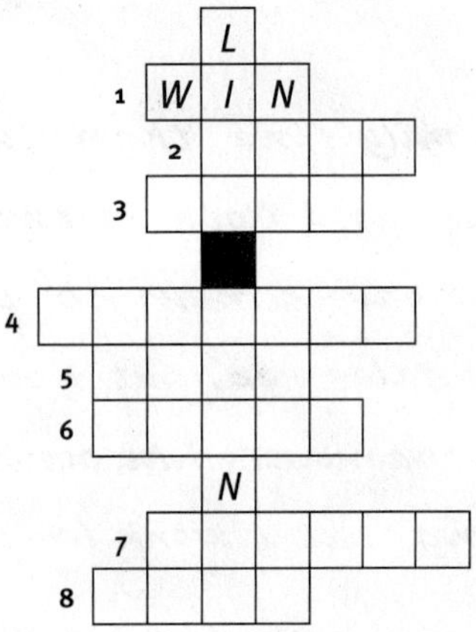

b Use phrases from Exercise 1a to label the pictures.

1. 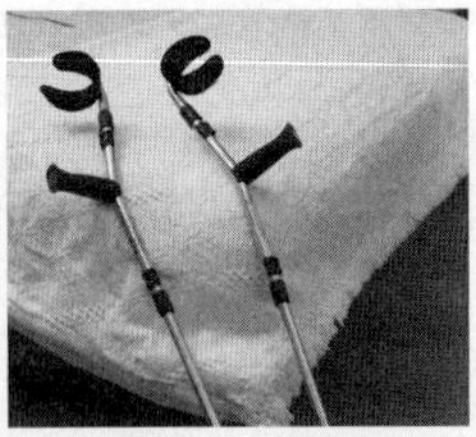

break your leg

2. 

____

3. 

____

4. 

____

Grammar

2 Complete the email with verbs from the box. Use the simple past.

walk	want	cook	~~start~~	listen
live	play	move	close	talk

to: lydia.fernandez@fastmail.com
from: irena_miller@epost.co.ca

Hello Lydia,

How are you? The weather here in Madrid is great. Our day *started* (**1.**) at 7:30 A.M. yesterday! Consuela ____________ (**2.**) breakfast for us. Then we ____________ (**3.**) to the Prado Gallery. Felipe ____________ (**4.**) to see the paintings by Goya and Velazquez. Felipe ____________ (**5.**) in Madrid when he was a child, but he ____________ (**6.**) to Canada when he was eight years old.

After lunch we ____________ (**7.**) tennis in the park. The park ____________ (**8.**) at 5:00 P.M. In the evening we ____________ (**9.**) to music and ____________ (**10.**) about our favorite singers at Consuela's house.

That's all for now. Send me an email and tell me your news!

Love,

Reina

3a Complete the article with the correct form of the verbs in parentheses.

Van Gogh's early life

Vincent Van Gogh *was* (1. be) born in The Hague in Holland in 1853. In 1869 he _______ (2. start) work. Van Gogh _______ (3. work) at an art firm. He _______ (4. not stay) in The Hague. In 1873 he _______ (5. move) to London. He _______ (6. love) a woman named Eugenie Loyer, but she _______ (7. not love) him. Van Gogh was very unhappy. He _______ (8. not like) his job, and in 1874 he moved to Paris. But Van Gogh _______ (9. not stay) in Paris . . .

b Use the cues to write questions and answers about Van Gogh.

1. (Van Gogh/move/London)
   A: *Did Van Gogh move to London*?
   B: Yes, *he did*.
2. (Van Gogh/love/Eugenie Loyer)
   A: _______________?
   B: Yes, _______________.
3. (Eugenie Loyer/love/Van Gogh)
   A: _______________?
   B: No, _______________.
4. (Van Gogh/like/his job)
   A: _______________?
   B: No, _______________.
5. (Van Gogh/stay/Paris)
   A: _______________?
   B: No, _______________.

Communication

4 Read the article. Then match the events to the dates.

This is a painting by Paul Gauguin. His full name was Eugene Henri Paul Gauguin. He was born in Paris on June 7, 1848. His family moved to Peru in 1849. In 1855 Gauguin moved back to France with his mother. Many people wonder, Was he friends with Vincent Van Gogh? It's an interesting question. He lived with Van Gogh for three months in 1888. But Gauguin didn't like Van Gogh and he didn't like Van Gogh's paintings. Gauguin moved to Tahiti, in 1895. His wife and children stayed in Europe. Gauguin didn't want to live in Europe, and he loved art from other countries. He worked in Tahiti, but it wasn't easy. He wasn't rich, he was very ill, and the police in Tahiti even arrested him! He died in 1903.

Events	Dates
e 1. Gauguin was born	a. 1855
___ 2. Gauguin moved to Peru	b. 1903
___ 3. Gauguin moved back to France	c. 1888
___ 4. Gauguin lived with Van Gogh	d. 1895
___ 5. Gauguin moved to Tahiti	~~e. 1848~~
___ 6. Gauguin died	f. 1849

Grammar

1a Complete the sentences with the simple past form of the verbs in parentheses.

1. Oliver and Emma *bought* (buy) a house in Mexico.
2. We __________ (go) to the movies last night.
3. You __________ (see) her. She was at the party.
4. Rachel __________ (say) no.
5. My manager and my wife __________ (meet) your daughter yesterday.
6. He __________ (give) an awful presentation yesterday.
7. Irena and I __________ (find) a beautiful hotel in the center of Kyoto.

b Complete the puzzle with the simple past form of the verbs. Some are regular and some are irregular. Find the secret phrase.

1. ~~play~~
2. win
3. lose
4. say
5. come
6. go
7. buy
8. find
9. finish
10. listen
11. meet

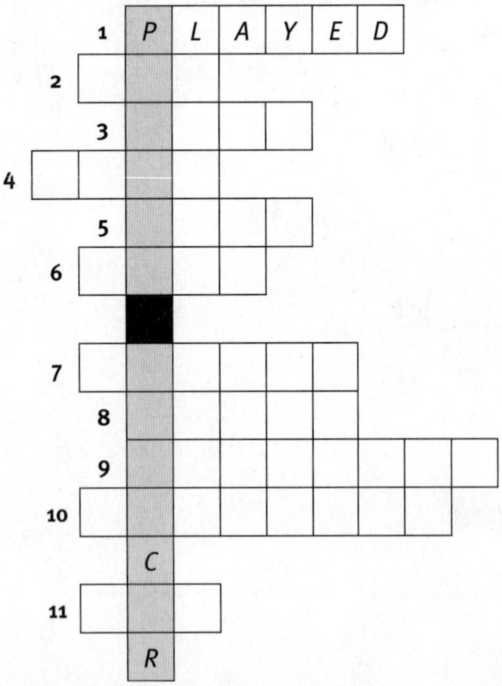

c Complete the article with the correct form of the verbs in parentheses.

Newlyweds win €15 million in Euro Lottery

Janice and Derek Parker from Cornwall *won* (**1.** win) €15 million in the Euro Lottery last week. Janice and Derek got married on Saturday morning. "We ________ (**2.** not go) on vacation," ________ (**3.** say) Janice. "We ________ (**4.** not have) any money. But we ________ (**5.** go) to a nice restaurant. In the evening I ________ (**6.** look) at the lottery numbers, and I ________ (**7.** be) so happy." And last Friday Derek ________ (**8.** buy) a present for Janice. What ________ (**9.** he/buy) for her? He ________ (**10.** not buy) a new car or a new house. He ________ (**11.** buy) a new dishwasher for her!

d Put the words in the correct order to make questions.

1. find/you/your/Did/wallet
   Did you find your wallet ?
2. Terry/go/out/night/Did/last
   ______________________________?
3. car/they/Did/a/buy/new
   ______________________________?
4. her/Did/love/you
   ______________________________?
5. to/Harry/London/Did/move
   ______________________________?
6. say/"Yes"/Did/you
   ______________________________?
7. lose/passport/you/on/Did/vacation/your
   ______________________________?
8. Did/lottery/win/we/the
   ______________________________?

Vocabulary

2 Write the numbers as spoken words.

1. 2,150 – _two thousand_ _one hundred_ and _fifty_
2. 1,010 – ________ ________ and ________
3. 980 – ________ ________ and ________
4. 15,612 – ________ ________ ________ ________ and ________
5. 9,999 – ________ ________ ________ ________ and ________-________
6. 86,321 – ________-________ ________ ________ ________ and ________-________
7. 115,200 – ________ ________ and ________ ________ ________ ________
8. 200,109 – ________ ________ ________ ________ ________ and ________

Communication

3 Write the words in parentheses as numbers.

Interesting facts

1. Mount Everest is _8,850_ (eight thousand eight hundred and fifty) meters tall.
2. About ________ (seven hundred and eighty thousand) people live in Dandong, China.
3. The Nile River is ________ (six thousand six hundred and fifty) kilometers long.
4. Jean Calment died in 1997. She was ________ (one hundred and twenty-two) years old.
5. There are fewer than ________ (ten thousand) red pandas in the world.
6. There are about ________ (six thousand nine hundred) languages in the world.

Writing

4 Rewrite the sentences in the correct order.

News story 1

A. He married Alexandre Serrano on his 81st birthday.
B. "Rio was very beautiful," he said, "but Alexandre is very, very beautiful."
C. He met her on vacation in Rio de Janeiro.
D. It was a good week for Cristiano Andrade from Portugal.

It was a good week for Cristiano Andrade from Portugal.
____
____
____

News story 2

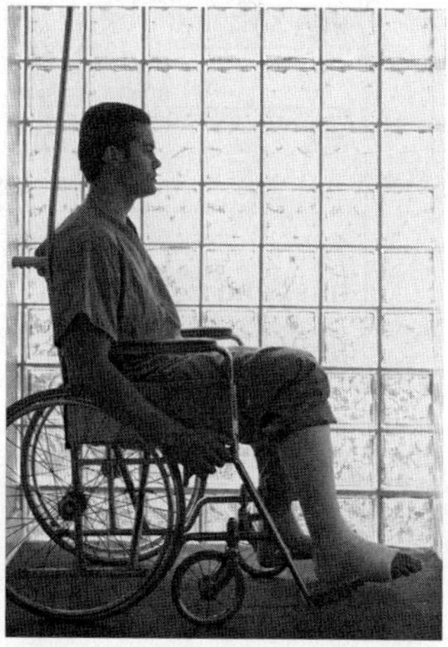

A. Now he can't play soccer for six months.
B. They bought soccer player Clive Lightfoot for $2.6 million.
C. Clive arrived at the soccer club on Monday morning.
D. It was a bad week for soccer team Rochdale United.
E. In the afternoon he broke his leg.

____
____
____
____
____

Grammar

1 Read the sentences. Then write another sentence. Use the verbs from the box and *be going to*.

find a new job	~~move~~
go to the beach	go to bed
break your leg	be rich
cook dinner tonight	

1. This country is cold. I *'m going to move*.
2. I went to bed late last night. I ______ early tonight.
3. Estelle doesn't like her job. She ______.
4. We are on vacation. We ______ this afternoon.
5. You can't ski. You ______.
6. He's a good businessman. He ______.
7. She's a great chef. ______.

2a Look at the chart. Complete the sentences about the people.

Winona and her family: Plans for next year		
	going to	not going to
me	eat a lot of vegetables	eat meat
my husband	work out	surf the Internet every evening
me and my husband	move	stay in our old house
my sister	get a new job	go out every night
my parents	travel	buy a new car

1. *I'm going to eat a lot of vegetables*.
   I'm not going to eat meat.
2. He ______.
   He ______.
3. We ______.
   We ______.
4. She ______.
   She ______.
5. They ______.
   They ______.

b Use the cues to write questions for Winona and her family.

1. (you/eat meat)
   Q: *Are you going to eat meat*?
   A: No, I'm not.
2. (your sister/get a new job)
   Q: *Is your sister going to get a new job*?
   A: Yes, she is.
3. (your parents/buy a new car)
   Q: ______?
   A: No, they're not.
4. (your husband/surf the Internet every evening)
   Q: ______?
   A: No, he's not.
5. (Where/you and your husband/move to)
   Q: ______?
   A: A big house near his parents.
6. (What job/your sister/get)
   Q: ______?
   A: She's going to be a chef.
7. (Where/your parents/travel to)
   Q: ______?
   A: They're going to travel to Japan and Korea.
8. (What activity/you and your husband/do)
   Q: ______?
   A: We're going to go hiking.

Communication

3 Read the answers. Then complete the questions.

1. A: *What are you going to do* next weekend?
   B: I'm not going to do anything next weekend. Why?
2. A: Why ______ learn Spanish?
   B: Because they want to live in Spain.
3. A: ______ a taxi?
   B: No, he isn't. He's going to take the bus.
4. A: ______ wash the dishes tonight?
   B: You are.
5. A: ______ on vacation next month?
   B: No, we aren't. We don't have any money.

Vocabulary

4a Match the verbs with the words to make phrases.

<u>d</u> **1.** learn	**a.** to college
____ **2.** have	**b.** a business
____ **3.** start	**c.** early
____ **4.** get	~~**d.** to drive~~
____ **5.** retire	**e.** a child
____ **6.** go	**f.** in shape

b Look at the pictures. What are the people going to do? Use the phrases from Exercise 4a and *be going to*.

1.

*He's going to learn to drive*______.

2.

______.

3.

______.

4.

______.

5.

______.

6.

______.

Reading

5 Read the article and answer the questions.

MAYA, a 34-year-old chef from Austin in Texas, loved to cook and wanted to have her own restaurant. But she didn't have any money. So what did she do? She had an idea—to compete on a TV cooking show. The prize? $100,000! So Maya made a videotape and sent it to the show. The tape showed her making pasta and lamb chops. The show asked Maya and 11 other chefs to come to Los Angeles. Maya competed against the other chefs—and she won!

So what is Maya going to do next? She's going to open an Italian restaurant in San Diego. Every day she's going to do what she loves: cook.

Congratulations, Maya!

1. What does Maya love to do?

______.

2. What did she want?

______.

3. What was her problem?

______.

4. What was the answer to her problem?

______.

5. What happened?

______.

6. Now what are Maya's plans?

______.

UNITS 7–10 Review

Imperatives

1 Match the words to make imperatives.

c 1. Sit	a. on, please.
___ 2. Turn	b. off your cell phone.
___ 3. Listen	c. ~~down, please.~~
___ 4. Be	d. at my emails.
___ 5. Hold	e. quiet, please.
___ 6. Don't come	f. in.
___ 7. Don't look	g. to me, please.

Adverbs of frequency

2 Rewrite the sentences with the adverbs.

1. I turn off my cell phone.
(never) *I never turn off my cell phone*.
2. I'm late.
(sometimes) ______________.
3. Do you work out?
(often) ______________?
4. Are they happy?
(always) ______________?
5. I have a coffee in the morning.
(usually) ______________.
6. She is early.
(not usually) ______________.

like + gerund/infinitive; *want* + infinitive

3 Use the cues to write sentences.

1. (Adriana/like/sing)
Adriana likes singing/Adriana likes to sing.
2. (Peter/want/go out tonight)
Does Peter want to go out tonight?
3. (My sister/not like/travel for work)
______________.
4. (Jose and Kay/not want/go swimming)
______________.
5. (Alan/not like/play golf)
______________.
6. (Sheila and Jeff/like/watch TV)
______________?
7. (I/not want/cook tonight)
______________.

Question words

4 Circle the correct question word.

1. *What/(Where)/Who* do you work?
2. *What/Where/Who* do you work for?
3. *What/Where/Who* music do you like?
4. *How/Which/Who* near is it?
5. *How/Which/Where* restaurant do you want to go to?
6. *What/Which/Where* do you do?

Simple past of *be*

5 Write questions. Use the past form of *be*.

1. (Where/he born)
Where was he born?
2. (What/their names)
______________?
3. (When/you a teacher)
______________?
4. (Where/she yesterday)
______________?
5. (When/your birthday)
______________?

Permission and requests

6 Complete the questions with *I* or *you*.

1. Can *you* spell that, please?
2. Could ______ use your computer?
3. Could ______ open the door for me?
4. Can ______ help you?
5. Could ______ listen to your Billie Holiday CD?
6. Can ______ sing me a song?

Dates

7 How do we say the dates below?

1. January 1 *January first*
2. 4/30 *April thirtieth*
3. 12/25 ______________
4. March 12 ______________
5. 11/13 ______________
6. July 4 ______________
7. 4/20 ______________
8. June 3 ______________

Simple past

8 Complete the sentences with verbs from the box in the simple past.

say	~~arrest~~	get	come	play	lose

1. The police *arrested* the art thief in the museum.
2. Louise ________ home at twelve o'clock last night.
3. I ________ my wallet last week. There was $30 and my credit cards in it.
4. I talked to my boss about a three week vacation, but he ________ no.
5. I went to bed late last night, and I ________ up late this morning.
6. Danny and Nina ________ tennis yesterday.

9 Complete the conversations with the simple past form of the verbs in parentheses.

1. A: When *did* the match *start*? (start)
   B: It *started* at three.
2. A: What ________ you ________ for lunch? (have)
   B: I ________ a salad.
3. A: Where ________ they ________ to? (move)
   B: They ________ to Australia, but they ________ ________ to Sydney.
4. A: ________ you ________ swimming? (go)
   B: We ________ ________ swimming. We ________ to the park.
5. A: What ________ you ________ in town? (buy)
   B: I ________ some clothes.
6. A: ________ Marlene ________ any photos of you. (take)
   B: No, she ________ But she ________ some pictures of Michael.
7. A: Where ________ Harry and Sally ________? (meet)
   B: They ________ in college.
8. A: Where ________ you ________ her? (see)
   B: I ________ her in a coffee shop on Hudson Street.

be going to

10 Use the cues to write complete sentences with *be going to.*

1. (I/not live at home)
   I'm not going to live at home.
2. (Samuel/learn to dance)
   ________________________.
3. (We/move to Seoul)
   ________________________?
4. (Mike and Danielle/not come to the wedding)
   ________________________.
5. (You/not cook dinner)
   ________________________?

Vocabulary

11 Complete the phrases with the verbs from the box. One verb is used twice.

move	go	break	learn	win
get	have	start	stay	

1. *break* your leg
2. ______ to college
3. ______ children
4. ______ married
5. ______ a business
6. ______ the lottery
7. ______ to a new country
8. ______ to swim
9. ______ in bed
10. ______ in shape

12 Match the word to make phrases.

h	1. factory	a. the theater
____	2. write	b. lab
____	3. main	c. out
____	4. go out	d. table
____	5. work	e. for work
____	6. go to	f. a meeting
____	7. coffee	g. to eat
____	8. travel	~~h. worker~~
____	9. research	i. reports
____	10. have	j. course

***English in Common* ActiveBook**
Installation Instructions

Windows

- Insert the disc into the CD-ROM drive of your computer. On most computers, the program will begin automatically.
- If the program does not begin automatically, open "My Computer."
- Right-click on the CD-ROM icon. Click on Open.

Macintosh

- Insert the disc into the CD-ROM drive of your computer.
- Double-click on the CD-ROM icon on your desktop.
- Double click on the "START_OSX" file to run the program. Leave the CD-ROM in the computer while using the program.

Note: You must have administrator privileges on the computer to install the program. To install:
- **Windows:** Double-click on the "install" file to start the installation.
- **Macintosh:** Copy all files from the CD-ROM to a folder on your hard drive.

ActiveBook System Requirements

	PC Compatible	Macintosh Compatible
Operating System	Microsoft Windows® XP, Vista, Windows 7	Mac OSX v. (10.4 & 10.5)
Processor	Intel Pentium® IV 1000MHz or faster processor (or equivalent)	PowerPC & Intel processor 500MHz or faster processor (or equivalent)
RAM	512 MB RAM minimum or higher	512 MB RAM minimum or higher
Internet Browser	Microsoft Internet Explorer® 7.x or Mozilla Firefox™ 4.x, or higher	Safari® 3.x, Mozilla Firefox™ 4.x, or higher
Plug-ins	Adobe PDF 8, Adobe Flash 9, or higher	Adobe PDF 8, Adobe Flash 9, or higher
Hardware	Computer CD-ROM drive, sound card and speakers or headphones	Computer CD-ROM drive, sound card and speakers or headphones
Monitor Resolution	1024x768	1024x768
Internet Connection	DSL, cable/broadband, T1, or other high-speed connection required to download plug-ins	

TECHNICAL SUPPORT

For Technical Product Support, please visit our support website at www.PearsonLongmanSupport.com. You can search our *Knowledgebase* for frequently asked questions, instantly *Chat* with an available support representative, or *Submit a Ticket/Request* for assistance.